1st US
REVIEW
COPY

45⁰⁰
LC

W9-BMH-021

WAGNER

a pictorial biography

WAGNER

a pictorial biography

BY WALTER PANOFSKY

A STUDIO BOOK

THE VIKING PRESS · NEW YORK

© Kindler Verlag 1963
Translated from the German by Richard Rickett
This edition © Thames and Hudson 1963
Published in 1964 by The Viking Press, Inc.
625 Madison Avenue, New York 10022 N.Y.
Library of Congress catalog card number 64-10447
Printed in Germany

'*A passion for the magic of Wagner has been part of my life ever since I first became aware of him and he began to take possession of me, to permeate my whole being. I can never forget how much enjoyment I owe to him, and how much I have learned from him too; nor can I ever forget those hours in the theatre alone in my rapture amid the vast audience, with every nerve, every fibre of my intellect thrilling with ecstasy at visions of great and moving import such as only this form of art can conjure up.*

'*In my mind's eye the spiritual stature of Richard Wagner is one of grandeur and suffering, like the nineteenth century of which it is the complete expression: furrowed in all its features, surcharged with all its diverse aspirations it appears before my eyes, and I am barely able to distinguish my love for his work, one of the most disputatious, enigmatical and fascinating phenomena in the whole creative world, from my love for the century of which his life spanned a great part, a life storm-tossed and restless, tormented, frenzied and misunderstood before emerging into the aura of world-wide renown.*'

THOMAS MANN

München, 17ten July 1865.

Am 22ten Mai 1813 in Leipzig geboren, zwei Tage darauf in der Thomaskirche mit dem Namen Wilhelm Richard getauft. Mein Vater Friedrich Wagner, zur Zeit meiner Geburt Polizei-actuarius in Leipzig, mit Anwartschaft auf die Stelle des Polizei-direktors daselbst, starb im Oktober des Jahres meiner Geburt in Folge grosser Anstrengungen, welche ihm die überhäuften polizeilichen Geschäfte während der Schlacht bei Leipzig zuzogen, durch Ansteckung des damals epidemisch gewordenen Nervenfiebers. Von seinem Vater vernahm ich späterhin dass er in dürftiger bürgerlicher Sphäre als Thoreinnehmer am Ranstädter Thore, sich dadurch von seinen Standesgenossen auszeichnete dass er seinen beiden Söhnen eine gelehrte Erziehung gab, indem er den einen — meinen Vater Friedrich Jurisprudenz, den andern, jüngern — Adolph, Theologie studieren liess. Mein Oheim gewann später einen nicht unbedeutenden Einfluss auf meine Entwickelung; wir werden ihn in einer entscheidenden Phase meiner Jugendgeschichte wieder begegnen. Über meinen für mich so früh verstorbenen Vater erfuhr ich später, dass

(Auf dem Brühl im "roth und weissen Löwen", zwei Treppen hoch)

Über die Lebensverhältnisse

'WHAT DID MY FATHER REALLY LOOK LIKE?' asked Siegfried, and the question may well have weighed on Wagner's own mind for the whole of his life, for it is by no means certain whether Friedrich Wagner, a police clerk, or a painter and actor named Ludwig Geyer was his real father. Until he was just over *His father* fourteen the boy retained the name of the man he so strikingly resembled, and it was not until Geyer's death that he reverted to the name of his mother's first husband. At that time the family returned from Dresden to Leipzig, where formerly people may well have indulged in a sly whisper or two at seeing the police clerk in the theatre night after night, ogling the *demoiselles* on the stage, while 'the brilliant actor took his place in the bosom of his family'.

It is not necessarily pure coincidence that not a single picture of Friedrich Wagner exists, whereas there is a picture of Richard's mother by Geyer, who also painted a number of self-portraits. It is definitely not pure coincidence that when Richard was dictating his life to Cosima von Bülow in his fifties he kept confusing the words 'father' and 'stepfather' whenever he was on the subject of Geyer. There is, too, the striking statement that he, Richard Wagner, could never escape the feeling that Ludwig Geyer's affectionate generosity to Friedrich Wagner's children was perhaps an attempt to atone for past sins.

Friedrich Wagner died six months after Richard's birth, and after a decent interval of one year Geyer married his friend's widow. Johanna Rosine, *née* Paetz, who had been brought up in a mill near Weissenfels, claimed to be the daughter of a Prince of Weimar, so on this side too there is uncertainty about Richard's descent.

From Wagner's autobiography *Mein Leben*

'*Zum roth und weissen Löwen*',
the house in Leipzig
where Wagner was born

Childhood experiences

The house where Richard was born, '*Zum roth und weissen Löwen*', *Auf dem Brühl* No. 3, was pulled down long ago. Nothing is left of his childhood home, which lacked parental control or any real family life. Even in these early years he felt drawn by the theatre, where Geyer played the villain and died a thousand deaths. At the age of five Richard submitted to being sewn into tights, equipped with wings, and appearing as an angel in an entertainment in honour of King Karl August of Saxony. In his schooldays he had his first speaking part in Kotzebue's *Menschenhass und Reue*. He was allowed to mime in charades at home on his parents' birthdays and was enraptured when in a Sappho parody he helped to draw Phaon's triumphal car. His complete absorption in the theatre dated from the day when he discovered Friedrich Wagner's puppet-theatre, for which he cut out figures, devised costumes and wrote high-flown dramas of knightly chivalry. At the age of twelve he was allowed to recite a Hamlet soliloquy before the whole class, and a poem he wrote on the death of a schoolfellow at the Kreuz school was actually printed.

His mother, Rosine Wagner

His stepfather,
Ludwig Geyer

His first complete literary effusion was a Teutonic tragedy called *Leubald und Adelaide*, written when he was fifteen. The heroine was named after a song by Beethoven, and the action was a hotchpotch of *Hamlet, Macbeth, King Lear, Richard III* and Goethe's *Götz von Berlichingen*. The mirth the piece gave rise to at home was attributed by Wagner to the lack of music, an omission which he forthwith proposed to rectify. Up till now he had done little but strum idly on the piano and develop a craze first for the *Ypsilanti Waltz* and later for the Huntsmen's Chorus from *Der Freischütz*. Now, however, he borrowed a book on the thorough-bass from Friedrich Wieck, 'the difficulties of which', to use his own words, 'were both a fascination and a challenge. I resolved to become a musician'.

Self-taught   At first he was entirely self-taught. He made fair copies of Beethoven's Fifth and Ninth Symphonies so as to find out for himself the art of scoring, and scraped away at a violin until he had acquired some knowledge of string instruments.

Christian Theodor Weinlig,
Wagner's first teacher

Wagner's first published composition

Much of his adolescence was a period of dilettantism and blind groping. His various moods were determined by the protagonists of his idealized artistic visions, in which the figures of Beethoven and Shakespeare merged into one. He followed many a false trail before, at the age of sixteen, he heard Wilhelmine Schröder-Devrient in *Fidelio* at the Leipzig Opera. He at once wrote to her, declaring categorically that she was an incomparable artist and the first person to give his life any meaning, and that if one day he should make a name for himself in the artistic world she should never forget that it was she alone who had made him what 'I hereby vow to become'. Wagner had found his Muse and he never forgot his oath.

There were many other youthful impressions that remained with him for the rest of his life. His journey to Prague on foot is echoed in his *Pilgerfahrt zu Beethoven*. The student's velvet cap which he took to in his fifties he had first admired at the age of eight.

Wagner's 'Muse',
Wilhelmine Schröder-Devrient

At nineteen, Wagner wrote
incidental music for *König Enzio*

Königl. Sächs. Hoftheater zu Leipzig.

Freitag, den 16. März, 1832.

König Enzio,

Historisches Trauerspiel in fünf Aufzügen,
von E. Raupach.

Die Ouverture und die Schluß-Musik im 5. Akte ist neu hierzu componirt von
Richard Wagner.

Personen:

Enzio, König von Sardinien, Kaiser Friedrich II. Sohn.	Herr Stölzel.
Ugone, Podesta von Bologna.	Herr Stein.
Geremei, Anziani von Bologna.	Herr Pögner.
Alberti,	Herr Köhler.
Lucia de Viadagoli, des Letzteren Nichte.	Dlle. Wagner.
Pietro degli Acinelli, deren Verwandter.	Herr Bünte.
Rainero de Gonfalenieri aus Piacenza.	Herr Linke.
Ein Gesandter König Konrad IV.	Herr v. Perglaß.
Filippo, Leichenpfleger.	Herr Reil.
Lamberto, Aufseher des Gefängnisses.	Herr Fischer.
Laura, Lucia's Vertraute.	Dlle. Tell.
Uberto, Enzio's Diener.	Herr Zimmermann.
Ein Hauptmann	Herr Saalbach.
	Herr Linde.
	Herr Schwarz.
Mehrere Anziani von Bologna.	Herr Grunow.
	Herr Gürtler.
	Herr Fischer jun.
Ein Soldat.	Herr Krebs.
Ein Leichenträger.	Herr Schumann.
Ein Begleiter des Gesandten.	Herr Koch.
Diener des Rathes. Träger und Soldaten.	

Ort und Zeit: Zu Bologna, im sechsten Jahrzehend des dreizehnten Jahrhunderts.

7. Vorstellung im fünften Monat - Abonnement.

Krank: Dlle. Sohm.

Preise der Plätze:

Parterre: 8 Groschen. Parket: 16 Groschen.
Logen des Parterres und Ersten Ranges: Ein einzelner Platz 16 Groschen.
Fremdenlege No. 25. 16 Groschen. Ein gesperrter Sitz daselbst 1 Thaler.
Logen des zweiten Ranges: Ein einzelner Platz 12 Groschen.
Fremdenlege No. 38. 8 Groschen. Ein gesperrter Sitz daselbst 16 Groschen.
Erste Gallerie: 12 Groschen. Ein gesperrter Sitz daselbst 16 Groschen.
Zweite Gallerie: 8 Groschen. Ein gesperrter Sitz daselbst 12 Groschen.
Dritte Gallerie: Mittelplatz 6 Groschen; Seitenplatz 4 Groschen.

Anfang um 6 Uhr.   Ende halb 9 Uhr.

Einlaß um 5 Uhr.

Sonntag, den 18. März: Neu einstudirt: Der politische
Zinngießer, Singspiel in zwei Aufzügen, von Treitschke.

On Christmas Eve 1830 Wagner secretly attended, not without gnawing apprehensions of disaster, the first performance of an extraordinary *Concert Overture* of his at the Leipzig Opera, a work he later referred to as the 'culmination of my follies'. In the following year he applied himself to his musical studies with redoubled zeal. Theodor Weinlig, a cantor at St Thomas's Church, knew well how to curb the exuberance of his unruly pupil. It is to him that Wagner's first published work, a *Sonata in B-flat major,* is dedicated. Wagner's incidental music to Raupach's *König Enzio* was first tried out anonymously and was so warmly received that at subsequent performances the name of the composer appeared on the play-bills. In the winter of 1832–33 a *Concert Overture in D minor* and a *Symphony in C major* were both performed at the Gewandhaus. His feet were already on the ladder.

For the time being, however, one aim and object overshadowed everything else – to be a student. Although still unmatriculated he behaved like a full-blooded fraternity member, gambling and drinking with his fellows and on one occasion, on an impulse he himself was unable subsequently to explain, surging with them into a brothel and carrying home like a triumphal banner, and a fetish too, a piece of dirty red curtain. And then he actually became a *studiosus musicae*, but he seemed less concerned with music than with showing what a terrific fellow he was. He struck up friendships with some of the most notorious duellists among the students and soon found himself involved in more than one challenge. This was the first of many occasions on which the lucky star under which Wagner was born appeared in the ascendant. Physically he was no match for his swashbuckling opponents and might well have been maimed for life if it had actually come to a duel, but his first opponent lost an arm in a students' bout a day or two before, and two others sneaked out of Leipzig to evade debts. A former friend with whom Wagner was also due to cross swords was killed in a duel with someone else, and when at last it was time for Wagner to fight his first duel his opponent had got so drunk the previous night that he was unable to compete.

Student

There was also another incident which confirmed his belief in his lucky star. He had become a great gambler, and on one occasion had even gambled away the whole of his mother's pension except for one last solitary taler. His first impulse was to flee the town at once, however ignominiously, but with a final fling he embarked on a run of luck that won back all his previous losses and enough to pay off all his debts besides. Overwhelmed by this evidence of Fortune's favour he abjured gambling for ever, and this was another vow that he never broke.

It was his mother who made it possible for him at the age of nineteen to visit Vienna; his luggage consisted of three *Concert Overtures* and his *Symphony in C*. In the old Imperial capital he admired Johann Strauss (father), was bored by Gluck's *Iphigenia in Aulis,* of which he was later to make a version of his own, and raved about Herold's *Zampa.* For the first, but by no means the last time he lived far beyond his means and the debts that he ran up in Vienna were still encumbering him during his days as Kapellmeister in Dresden. On the way home he stopped at Prague to visit one or two girls he had known in his younger days, and secretly completed a libretto for a romantic opera *Die Hochzeit* (The Wedding) which anticipated *Lohengrin* in many ways, including a decision by ordeal and a procession to church. But neither the libretto nor the first sketches of the music found favour with 'Geistchen', as Ludwig Geyer used to call Richard's sister Rosalie, whom in those days he absolutely adored. A second project, this time completed, met with Rosalie's whole-hearted approval, and from Gozzi's fable *La donna serpente* Wagner completed his first opera, *Die*

First stay in Vienna

Feen (The Fairies), in January 1834. During the preparations for its first performance at the Leipzig Opera a dispute arose between the management, who provided turbans and caftans, and Wagner, who demanded the 'knightly apparel of the earliest Middle Ages'.

Before *Die Feen* was performed he was already planning a second opera, *Das Liebesverbot* (Ban on Love). Influenced by Heinse's novel *Ardinghello*, Wagner turned to Shakespeare's *Measure for Measure* and in glorification of his ideal of 'unrestrained sensuality' turned the comedy into a grisly drama which he later smilingly dismissed as 'a curious mix-up': it started with the storming of a brothel in Palermo!

To avoid having to start on the arduous business of preparing *Die Feen*
during the hot summer months, Kapellmeister Stegmayer of the Leipzig Opera
recommended Wagner to apply forthwith for the post of Director of the Magdeburg *Theatergesellschaft*. Wagner set off at once for Lauchstädt, to the little
wooden theatre which had been built to a design by Goethe and had staged
the first performance of Schiller's *Braut von Messina* and was now being
desecrated for a summer season by a fifth-rate troupe from Magdeburg run by
Heinrich Bethmann, with only one performer of any pretensions, Minna
Planer.

Up till now Wagner's relations with the opposite sex had amounted to nothing
more than one or two injudicious infatuations. In 1833, when he was chorus-
master of the Würzburg Opera with a monthly salary of ten gulden, he had
fallen seriously in love with a grave-digger's daughter whose outward appearance 'stimulated my fancy most agreeably'. But the budding relationship
was severed just as it was on the point of being legalized. A second *affaire*
occasioned Wagner his first twinge of 'self-confident complacency'. Without

The theatre at Lauchstädt

undue difficulty he relieved an oboe-player of his fiancée, a certain Fräulein Galvani, danced with her to the oboist's tune with an exuberance that was positively provocative, and fired by wine conducted himself with the girl 'like any other happy pair'. The *affaire* was never more than 'a charming adventure', yet it was not without significance: from now on Wagner, though almost a dwarf in stature, was well aware of his attraction for women.

Minna Planer

Minna Planer, 'leading tragédienne' of the Magdeburg troupe, was an actress of necessity rather than by inclination. At the age of fifteen she had been seduced by a Count and since then she had been accompanied on her travels by her 'sister' Natalie who was in reality her daughter. She made good use of her outstanding personal charms to provide for her parents as well as her daughter as an actress. If Minna was anything but a bohemian, neither was she, as Wagner was soon to find out, by any means the ideal, unapproachable and virtuous creature he had supposed. As the Fairy Amorosa in Nestroy's *Lumpazi vagabundus* she struck him as a woman who had little in common with theatrical folk. From the moment he first encountered her in the doorway of the theatre

The theatre at Magdeburg

The earliest portrait
of the composer

he was all hers. At each successive meeting she became more and more the goal
of the passionate aspirations that *Ardinghello* and *Liebesverbot* had kindled in
him. At first Minna resisted Wagner's advances, though not unkindly. Yet she
may well have reckoned that a man who at his tender age (four years younger
than she) was already an operatic director would surely one day be able to
provide her with the security she so sorely craved. One evening in 1835 Wagner
drank himself into a stupor in Minna's bedroom. She let him have her bed
'wherein I slept until that wondrous dawn which, as I perceived where I lay,
ushered in for me with growing and unmistakable clarity the awareness of a

life-partnership which from that very morning was to be of long and infinitely fateful consequence'.

There has been a deal of speculation on the relationship between Minna and Richard. But the explanation of their partnership, however strained it may have been, is perfectly simple: Wagner more or less capitulated to Minna because she was the first woman in his life. When during the early days of their acquaintance she continued to be on friendly terms with a young aristocrat, Richard soon had occasion to learn how much more experienced she was than he,

Minna Planer,
Wagner's first wife

a realization which induced a certain inferiority complex later sublimated in gratitude. Wagner had foreseen what was coming and had been unable to evade it. From that morning on he was tortured by the thought that he was not the only man in Minna's life. 'You are all my life; do not forget me, do not deceive me; be true to me, always be *my* Minna, and whenever you feel in need of love turn wholly and completely to me and never let me have to share you with anyone.'

But Minna kept Wagner in suspense. When the Magdeburg season came to an end and they had to part it was he who thirsted for some token of love. He wrote long and ardent letters, once cramming over five thousand words on to two sheets in order to save postage. Minna, on tour with 'sister' Natalie, did nothing about seeing him again. Despite her excellent connections in the theatrical world, during her engagement in Königsberg she hardly lifted a finger to help her secret suitor. And she was still far from making up her mind one way or the other: debts and starvation were not at all what she wanted and his blind jealousy got on her nerves. Yet she continued to listen to what he had to say.

It was in Königsberg that the decision was at last taken, and they were married on 24 November 1836, the only witnesses being one or two people from the theatre. Wagner hardly heard the priest's words: 'At this moment it became clear to me as in a vision that my whole being was divided into two separate currents bearing me along in diametrically opposite directions: the upper current, aspiring to the sun, bore me onward as in a dream, while the lower one held me in the grip of a profound and inexplicable apprehension.'

Playbill of one of Minna Wagner's appearances at the Riga *Stadttheater*

The *Rule, Britannia Overture*, first performed in Riga on 2 March 1838

Wagner's misgivings were well-founded. Six months after the wedding Minna left him and went off with a 'protector', first to Dresden and then all over Germany, until she was finally abandoned by him in a Hamburg lodging-house. Wagner toyed with the idea of divorce but with Minna's letter confessing her guilt and asking forgiveness his anger turned to self-reproach. No divorce. 'All that lives in me is a single ardent desire, a longing that is counting the minutes till I can hold you in my arms again.'

Wagner's musical activities were remarkably unaffected by all these happenings. He composed an overture based on *Rule, Britannia,* and a chance reading of Bulwer Lytton's *Rienzi* gave him an idea for a new opera.

At Riga

His centre of gravity was now Riga, where the Opera Director Karl von Holtei was looking for a straightforward piece of the *Singspiel* type. Wagner, however, deliberately continued work on *Rienzi,* well aware that it was not a work he could ever hope to see staged save at one of the great opera houses of Europe. Never again would he risk such a ghastly *débâcle* as the benefit performance of *Liebesverbot* at Magdeburg.

Minna's return to her husband cost her her career on the stage. From now on she was the good housewife, 'cooking *Bratwurst* or omelettes or leg of mutton with cheese'. But this domestic bliss did not last long: Holtei resigned, Wagner's contract expired, and with his creditors growing uneasy about their money – by now Wagner himself had no idea how much he owed – there was only one course open, to slip away.

Work on Rienzi

As he worked at *Rienzi* Wagner had come to realize that in Riga he was completely cut off from the musical world. A great city like Paris must have seemed like a beckoning mirage, the only place that could set his feet on the road to fame. Accordingly he wrote off to Scribe and Meyerbeer and although he never received an answer he was happy 'to be in touch with Paris'. And when he heard that his younger sister Cäcilie had settled there with her husband Eduard Avenarius it seemed to him like the finger of fate. Plans were laid to sneak away, and Wagner and Minna finally saw the last of Riga in July 1839. They were not alone: 'Robber', an enormous Newfoundland dog, had attached himself to them in Riga and followed them about devotedly.

Flight from creditors

After managing to slip across the Russo-Prussian frontier they had an accident: the coach overturned at Pillau and Minna had a miscarriage. Eventually, without passports, they embarked on a small sailing-vessel named *Thetis*, the captain being a respectable smuggler, a *Daland*. Day after day their voyage to London was protracted by head-winds and violent storms, with no shelter till they reached the Norwegian fjords. Before *Rienzi* was anywhere near finished the eerie experiences of the voyage were beginning to crystallize in the form of a new opera based on the tale of 'The Flying Dutchman', which Wagner had recently come across in Heinrich Heine's *Memoiren des Herrn von Schnabelewopski*. The calls and songs of the sailors, the tearing of the wind, the St Elmo's fire in the rigging at night: both the story and the music began to take shape.

In essence, the libretto of the new opera was simply the expression of Wagner's constant meditations on the subject of Minna. In a letter dated as early as 1836 he dreams of her as of a woman, faithful and loving, who will follow him to the ends of the earth, and let the world think what it will. Senta is the Minna that Wagner idealized and he himself is the Dutchman, driven ever onward, who can only be freed from the curse of the past by the love of a woman.

The perils of the voyage had for the time being strengthened the bonds of marriage: on one desperate occasion Minna had asked to be tied to her husband so that they could go to their watery graves together. Wagner's attentions to his young wife were touching, and she repaid them by her cleverness in converting the meagre resources at their disposal into the comforts that Richard, who at heart was of a home-loving disposition, so badly needed.

During the fruitless search in London for Bulwer Lytton, author of *Rienzi*, Wagner's bland importunity – his own expression was 'resolute urgency' – secured him a seat for a session of the House of Lords. He also travelled in a steamship for the first time in his life. Then they pressed on to France, where the optimism with which they had started out suddenly gave way to premonitions of gloom. And in fact from the very first they were both duped by their blind trust in themselves and their fellow-men. With inexplicable whole-heartedness Wagner had relied on the help of Meyerbeer. He was firmly convinced that such a great man would surely come to the aid of a kindred spirit. When in due course Meyerbeer, the 'musical Pope' of France who had Europe at his feet, received him with characteristic French courtesy, in Boulogne, Wagner was in the seventh heaven. In Meyerbeer's letters of recommendation he already saw practical results and he was bemused by the very sound of the name 'Paris'. *In Paris* He felt like a young eagle whose wings had grown again after being severely clipped in Riga. Finding in the Rue de la Tonnellerie a cheap hotel at which Molière was said to have been born, Wagner, who was always gullible in such matters, took this too as a good omen.

Giacomo Meyerbeer, the 'musical Pope' of his day

First residence in Paris: the hotel
in the Rue de la Tonnellerie

He was much mistaken. Some new acquaintances and vague promises were all that came his way, yet his self-confidence was unimpaired. He was still able to pay the hotel bill, and he counted on help from his sister and her husband. It was Minna who took him in hand when at last his eyes were opened. For a time Wagner still believed he had only to sit down and compose an aria or two for the money to come rolling in, but his music remained unheard; it was not the kind of music Paris liked. Enquiries had to be made as to the whereabouts of the nearest pawnbroker and some silver disposed of. And in October 1840 he was sent to prison for debt.

For the rest of his life Wagner looked upon these days as one long humiliation. Ten years after his first farewell to Paris he took his revenge with a philosophical treatise directed against Meyerbeer and all the other Jews who had crossed his path there. And in old age he still cursed Paris as 'a pit into which the real spirit of a whole nation has subsided'.

The Wagners moved from the Molière hotel to a small town house. It was Richard's intention to finish *Rienzi*, instead of which he found himself making arrangements of Donizetti and Halévy for piano solo and duet, quartet, *cornets à pistons* and two violins. He was working for Maurice Schlesinger, whose niggling accuracy in money matters was construed by the liberal Wagner as dishonesty. Schlesinger assessed Wagner's work by the line with a device of his own invention and arrived at far less magnificent sums than the fees Wagner had originally demanded, and probably already spent.

What for Wagner may well have been even more galling than being materially dependent on a calculating business-man was the fact that he was handling music that he heartily despised. As he grew older his conception of the Franco-Italian idiom as a sin against the whole spirit of opera hardened. And now here he was having to keep the wolf from the door by making popular arrangements of the very works he so abominated.

Paris hotel bill

So far he had not earned a penny by composition, and it was not until near the end of his time in Paris that his song *Dors, mon enfant* brought in a modest fee. He had his setting of Heine's *Die beiden Grenadiere*, with the *Marseillaise* ingeniously woven into the accompaniment, engraved at his own expense, paying off the fifty francs that Schlesinger charged him for it by articles and short stories. As Wagner knew no French half the fee, already by no means princely, went to the translator.

However, the whole of the *Dutchman* libretto was already sketched and *Rienzi* fully scored by 19 November 1840. Wagner never worked harder than in these Paris days, and perhaps his toil never again seemed so futile: he had long ago recognized that Paris was not the place for him. The dream that he had dreamed in Riga was over, and all his hopes turned to Dresden, where he knew his 'Muse' Wilhelmine Schröder-Devrient, and Tichatschek, in whom he saw the ideal Rienzi. So the score of *Rienzi*, the bulkiest Wagner ever produced, was sent off to Dresden. For more than a year all Wagner's hopes were reposed on it, for his friends, especially the painter Kietz, had no regular incomes to support even themselves. The state of the Wagners' finances, primarily at Minna's instigation, was always carefully kept from their relatives, even if they had to demean themselves in the eyes of the *concierge* by cleaning the boots of the lodger they had taken in the hope of making ends meet.

Not surprisingly, the atmosphere was often explosive. A poem Wagner hastily scribbled as a peace-offering after a domestic mishap – a chair had split in two – shows what trifling incidents could provoke a quarrel. Wagner signed the poem with a caricature of himself: in those days to save the cost of shaving he had a beard, which gave him a curiously gnome-like appearance.

In order to be free to work on the score of the *Dutchman* he sold the

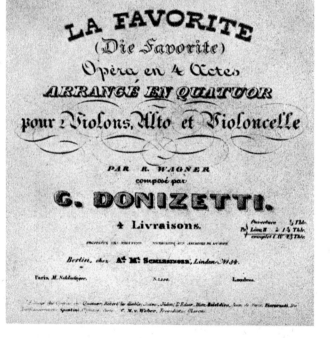

Title page of a Donizetti arrangement

From the Paris days:
an apology to Minna signed
with a caricature by himself

sketch of the libretto to the Director
of the Grand Opera, Léon Pillet, for
five hundred francs. The score was
fully sketched in seven weeks, and
then Wagner had to arrange Halévy's
latest success *La reine de Chypre* for
Schlesinger.

For all the apparent cordiality of
his encounter with the composer of
La Juive Wagner saw no reason to follow it up. Life seemed so unfair: what
Wagner failed to produce even after
the most desperate exertions seemed
to pour forth from Halévy with effort-
less ease. Nor did Halévy appear to
appreciate that an artist's most important qualification (in Wagner's
view) was a glowing belief in the mission of Art. It was contact with Halévy that gave Wagner his first concrete ideas for his pamphlet *Judaism
in Music*.

His meeting with Hector Berlioz
was equally unproductive. The composer of the *Symphonie Fantastique*
had read Wagner's story *Eine Pilgerfahrt zu Beethoven* (A Pilgrimage to
Beethoven) in the *Gazette Musicale*
and expressed his admiration of it to
Schlesinger. Whereupon Wagner called on him with *Die beiden Grenadiere* under his arm, but Berlioz was
unable to manage the piano part:
according to Wagner all he could do
was strum a few notes on the guitar.

The *Gazette Musicale*, in which Wagner's *Pilgerfahrt zu Beethoven* appeared

The *Pilgerfahrt* was followed by the remarkable tale *Ein Ende in Paris* (An End in Paris). Once again the story contained much that was autobiographical, the dog Robber, who mysteriously disappeared in Paris and then turned up again like a ghost, playing an important part. More important are passages like the following: 'I need hardly enumerate the details which extinguished my confidence and enthusiasm except to state that it was not rocks on which I foundered: fortunate indeed is the mariner who is wrecked in a storm! No: it was in a bog, a morass, that I went under.' 'You see me beaten down: suffice it to say that it was not on the battle-field but — and this is a terrible thing to say — to the pangs of hunger in waiting-rooms that I succumbed.' And finally: 'This is my final creed. I believe in God, Mozart and Beethoven, and likewise in their disciples and followers. I believe in the Holy Ghost and in the truth of a single, indivisible Art. I believe that this Art proceeds from God and lives in the hearts of all men of enlightenment. I believe that whoever has once savoured the exquisite joys of this Art must for ever be its devoted servant and can never repudiate it. And I believe that through this Art all men shall be blessed.'

On 12 April 1842, after two and a half years of drudgery in Paris, Wagner arrived at Dresden with Minna. *Rienzi* was about to be put on there, and the *Flying Dutchman* in Berlin. It was the generosity of his brother-in-law Avenarius that made the move to Dresden possible, a Christmas (1841) goose with a 500 franc note in its beak.

In Dresden

Wagner, a pencil drawing
by E. B. Kietz, 1842

The Royal Court Theatre in Dresden

The one solitary hour of sunshine during the five-day journey vouchsafed Wagner a glimpse of the Wartburg, which immediately inspired him as the set for the third act of the new opera he was planning, *Tannhäuser*. He had come upon the story purely by chance, while collecting material for an opera about the Hohenstaufen dynasty to be called *Die Sarazenin*, in a book of popular legends containing the Venusberg saga, where the Tournament of Song on the Wartburg was loosely associated with the Tannhäuser saga that Wagner already knew from Ludwig Tieck's *Phantasus*. Further possibilities were suggested by a publication of the German Society of Königsberg, which incidentally also discussed the Lohengrin epic.

For the time being, however, all Wagner's efforts were concentrated on *Rienzi*. His powers of persuasion worked wonders: no trace now of the abject defeatism of *Ein Ende in Paris*, even though the Wagners lived on a very modest scale and subsisted mainly on 'potatoes and herrings'. The tenor Joseph

Tichatschek, who was not exactly overburdened with intelligence, was won over by the prospect of appearing in silver armour. The 'Muse' was by this time certainly beginning to look her age, and her 'motherly embonpoint' was hardly the best qualification for the rôle of Adriano, but now for the first time Wagner displayed his remarkable ability as a producer. With infinite tact and patience he secured performances from both tenor and *prima donna* which though not completely satisfying him cemented a lifelong association with both of them.

Rienzi was performed for the first time on 20 October 1842, though there had not been a single uninterrupted dress rehearsal. The performance was advertised to start at six and end at ten o'clock, but by ten it had only got as far as

Playbill of the first performance of *Rienzi*

Wagner's occasional composition *At Weber's Grave*

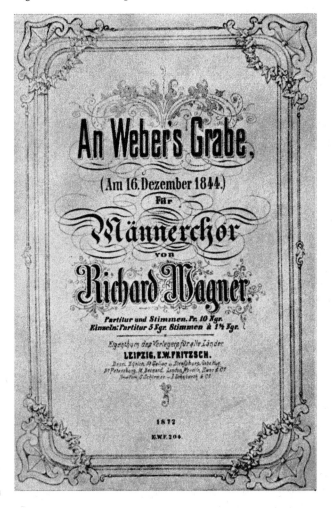

the end of Act III and it was midnight before Wagner came on to the stage to acknowledge the storms of applause.

The events of the following day are a tragi-comedy almost without parallel: worried lest *Rienzi's* inordinate length should jeopardize its further success, Wagner went round to the copyist's office and made a series of slashing cuts which Tichatschek and Fischer, the chorus master, promptly restored. At the suggestion of the Intendent, von Lüttichau, the work was then divided into two, *Rienzi's Greatness* and *Rienzi's Fall*, but the public protested against this act of mutilation and in the end the work was given at a single performance with one or two cuts, and each time it was a prodigious success.

Minna was even more delighted than Richard. Here at last were the great days her husband had promised her, and when Wagner was offered the post of Kapellmeister which had suddenly fallen vacant her joy knew no bounds. She could not understand why he hesitated, and in fact his attitude is not easy to account for. It may be that the salary, 1,500 taler a year, seemed too small; more probably Wagner could see what was going to happen if he accepted. And in fact scarcely had the news of his appointment appeared in the *Gazette* than the new Court Kapellmeister was deluged with I.O.U's from earlier years. Wagner extricated himself from this situation with his usual dexterity. All his life he was in trouble over money, and all his life he found people only too ready to lend or give him some. He was in debt till his dying day, but in later years he managed to realize his ambition of leading a life of affluence. It was not so much Minna as Caroline, the widow of Carl Maria von Weber, who succeeded in persuading Wagner to accept the post previously occupied by her husband, and Wagner was appointed Court Kapellmeister 'for life'.

Until he took up this post on 2 February 1843 Wagner's life had been one long struggle to make ends meet. As a musician he was virtually unknown, excluded from 'Society' and constrained to go about with people like the painter Kietz who for all their sincerity and affection would never amount to anything in the world. Now he was no longer a nobody. Now he was looked up to by Society and about to find that an artistically-minded aristocracy was ready to attest its esteem and understanding. The out-and-out bourgeois who would not compose unless his little dog Peps was lying by the piano and who insisted on being greeted by the parrot Papo before he had crossed the threshhold now carried on long conversations with Ida von Lüttichau. Her influence on him was 'considerable, consolidating my personal pride'. 'This sensitive woman, pining away in an environment of the utmost vulgarity', stood by him when the *Flying Dutchman* came up against 'lack of understanding', and it was to her, for attempting to understand his 'swimming against the current', that the new opera was dedicated. Minna's first rival had appeared on the scene, a member of high society, an artistically-minded and beautiful woman far above bourgeois habits of thought.

Dresden was selected for the first performance of the *Flying Dutchman* even before the première of *Rienzi*. The scenery was allocated as early as 24 September 1842: the cyclorama for Act I was borrowed from *Oberon*, as were the masts of the ships, though the hulls came from a ballet called *Der Seeräuber*. Gretchen's room in *Faust* was made over for Senta, and for Act III a house from the play *William Tell* was requisitioned.

It was in these borrowed plumes that the *Flying Dutchman* was given its first performance on 2 January 1843. It was Wagner's first encounter with the world of legend, and its consequences were more apparent in the action than in the music, which still adheres to the established pattern of individual numbers, though the *motif* idea is already beginning to make itself heard. The figure of the Dutchman is compounded of the wandering Odysseus, the wandering Jew, and the great sixteenth-century explorers. Wagner, who had once paid tribute to Columbus with an Overture, always saw himself as an explorer too, so that

The Wagner house at Graupa

Stage-set for the first performance of the *Flying Dutchman*

1ste Vorstellung im vierten Abonnement.

Königlich Sächsisches Hoftheater.

Montag, den 2. Januar 1843.
Zum ersten Male:

Der fliegende Holländer.

Romantische Oper in drei Akten, von Richard Wagner.

Personen:

Daland, norwegischer Seefahrer.	Herr Risse.
Senta, seine Tochter.	Mad. Schröder-Devrient.
Erik, ein Jäger.	Herr Reinhold
Mary, Haushälterin Dalands.	Mad. Wächter.
Der Steuermann Dalands.	Herr Bielezizky.
Der Holländer.	Herr Wächter.

Matrosen des Norwegers. Die Mannschaft des fliegenden Holländers. Mädchen.
Scene: Die norwegische Küste.

Textbücher sind an der Casse das Exemplar für 2½ Neugroschen zu haben.

Playbill of the first performance of the *Flying Dutchman*

Scene from the first
performance of *Tannhäuser*

Wagner's niece Johanna as Elisabeth

Playbill of the first performance of *Tannhäuser*

The inn 'Zur Eiche'
at Teplitz-Schönau

in the *Flying Dutchman*, as in all his earlier works, there is an autobiographical element. And it was in Senta that he found what he looked for in vain in Minna: 'the as yet non-existent, yearned for, dreamed of and infinitely womanly woman', the 'woman of the future who will bring redemption'. As to what the *Flying Dutchman* really is Wagner was far less clear when he was actually engaged in writing the text of this mythical vision than he was in later years, when he characterized its action and its figures in his *Communication to my friends*. The step from opera to music-drama was a halting one: the process was more unconscious than otherwise. It is only later that it becomes apparent how logically one work leads to the next.

Wagner was now getting through a prodigious amount of work. In the Opera he was conducting almost the whole repertoire, including the Italian works. An association with a choral society meant more work, including the *Liebesmahl der Apostel* (Love Feast of the Apostles) and hymns for ceremonial acts of homage to the King. There was music to be composed for the occasion of the bringing home from London (on Wagner's instigation) of the body of Carl Maria von Weber. He also undertook a rearrangement of Gluck's *Iphigenia*, elucidating the action and altering the instrumentation.

As regards his own work, *Tannhäuser* was taking shape. Some of the music had already been sketched at an inn named 'Zur Eiche' at Teplitz-Schönau, but the real inspiration was still to come. Meanwhile Wagner had completed his *Venusberg* poem – a title that had no hope whatever of passing the censor – on his thirtieth birthday: he loved symbolic coincidences of this kind.

Wagner's arrangement of Gluck

Once again it was Wilhelmine Schröder-Devrient who provided the decisive stimulus to the composition of *Tannhäuser*. 'As for true love, I noticed in the case of a woman I admired that the same kind of urges as mine could imagine themselves satisfied only by the most trivial encounters, so that the element of folly could never really be kept hidden from the urge.' The 'Muse' had given up a lover of many years' standing for a new one who looked like ruining her. 'What could a longing for love, the noblest emotion my being can experience, be other than a desire to be transported from the present, to die away into an element of endless love here on earth, the kind of love that seems only attainable in death?'

First performance of Tannhäuser

On 13 April 1845 the score was completed and the work was performed for the first time on 19 October with Tichatschek as Tannhäuser, the 'Muse' as Venus and Wagner's niece Johanna as Elisabeth. The well-meaning audience of Dresden was somewhat at a loss, and Wagner himself was disappointed, realizing only too clearly that with the performers and theatrical amenities at his disposal his visionary ideals were unobtainable. Yet he was sure of himself: 'If this work is not good, I shall never do any good.'

Wagner had been Court Kapellmeister for over six years when he was compelled to flee as a result of his activities during the May insurrection of 1849.

The May uprising in Dresden

Was he really in his heart of hearts a revolutionary? With Wagner one keeps on coming up against curious contradictions but they at once resolve themselves if his activities are judged by the single criterion that governed his whole life. Wagner was an out-and-out egoist: his work meant everything to him, and where his artistic ideals were concerned morality, convention, freedom and love were of no account. For his work's sake he rushed to the barricades, embraced a king, renounced all he had preached.

Michael Bakunin, a ringleader of the May uprising in Dresden

For his work's sake he surrounded himself with people whom he needed, and disowned them when neither he nor his work had any further use for them.

It is from this aspect that Wagner's part in the 1849 revolution must be looked at. As an adolescent he had joined in the seditious clamour of Leipzig students without really knowing what it was all about. Now he favoured his friend the chorus-master August Röckel, who was important for his work, with a display of interest in his political visions. His acquaintance with Michael Bakunin, one of the real founders of communism, bore an element of recklessness, since Bakunin was under police surveillance. It was, of course, characteristic of Wagner to regard with esteem and approval a man who after a performance of Beethoven's Ninth which, under Wagner's baton, sounded as if it had just been rediscovered, rushed up to the conductor, heedless of police spies, and declared that if every note of music ever written were to be destroyed in the coming world conflagration this work must be saved even at the peril of their lives.

Politisch gefährliche Individuen.

Richard Wagner
ehemal. Kapellmeister und politischer Flüchtling aus Dresden.

Die Nr. 140 der „Leipziger Zeitung" vom 20. Mai 1849 brachte folgenden Original-

Steckbrief.

Der unten etwas näher bezeichnete Königl. Capellmeister

Richard Wagner von hier ist wegen wesentlicher Theilnahme an der in hiesiger Stadt stattgefundenen aufrührerischen Bewegung zur Untersuchung zu ziehen, zur Zeit aber nicht zu erlangen gewesen. Es werden daher alle Polizeibehörden auf denselben aufmerksam gemacht und ersucht, Wagnern im Betretungsfalle zu verhaften und davon uns schleunigst Nachricht zu ertheilen.

Dresden, den 16. Mai 1849.

Die Stadt-Polizei-Deputation.

von Oppell.

Wagner ist 37—38 Jahre alt, mittler Statur, hat braunes Haar und trägt eine Brille.

Die Nr. 42 des „Koburger Allgem. Polizei-Anzeigers" vom 29. Mai 1849 brachte unter der Rubrik „Steckbriefe" Folgendes:

„Wagner, Rich., k. Kapellmeister aus Dresden; Alter: 38 Jahre; Statur: mittel; Haare: braun; trägt eine Brille."

Dieser Steckbrief ward unter der Ueberschrift: „Staats-

Wagner was far too much of an egoist and individualist ever to have practised these ideals. Like many of his contemporaries, he dreamed of a democracy presided over by a king, and it was the king, not the masses, who should have the final word. When he spoke of the necessity of changing existing conditions it was *his* world, not *the* world, that he wanted improved. He fretted at being dependent on the Court camarilla and officials: in his view only the king had the right to decide artistic questions. It was when his pamphlet on the reorganization of the theatre (from which the only person to benefit would be Wagner himself) fell on deaf ears and von Lüttichau failed to display much interest in *Lohengrin* that his revolutionary fervour was aroused. He was perhaps a fellow-traveller who imagined he was fighting for certain ideals when in reality it was himself and his own work that came first.

For one who observed the progress of the revolution from the tower of the *Kreuzkirche*, ubiquitous and elusive, and who had expressed his views on political developments in speeches and pamphlets, there was only one course open when the revolution fizzled out. By way of Chemnitz and Altenburg he eventually came to Weimar, and so to Franz Liszt.

Wagner had been introduced to this celebrated figure in his Paris days but had never succeeded in making much of an impression. After the success of *Rienzi* Wilhelmine Schröder-Devrient brought the two men together again with diabolical glee, telling Liszt that in his indefatigable pursuit and encouragement of talent he had missed a budding genius. From then on the ties that bound Liszt and Wagner were never severed, for they both possessed the faculty of attracting kindred spirits to themselves.

Liszt's care for the fugitive with a warrant out against him was touching. There was only one worry he was unable to relieve Wagner of: Minna. She was quite bewildered at finding the life she had so laboriously built up shattered overnight, all her dreams evaporated. Her letters during this time are full of reproaches: she had no intention of playing the tragic rôle of an abandoned wife. She set off apprehensively after her husband to Zürich.

Certain to be arrested in any German State, Wagner had managed to get to Switzerland on a false (and out-of-date) passport. The journey had been financed by Liszt on the security of royalties from *Lohengrin*. The old epic which Wagner had first come across in Paris suddenly came back to him as he was doing a cure at Marienbad, where immediately after putting the finishing touches to *Tannhäuser* he made the first prose sketches for *Die Meistersinger*, which was meant to act as a sort of satiric complement to the Wartburg Tournament of Song. Within three weeks the rough sketch of *Lohengrin* was finished and a year later the music was also sketched. Work on the orchestration was not parallel with the action: Act III was done first, followed by Act I, Act II, and finally the Prelude.

A month after the first performance of *Tannhäuser* Wagner had given a reading of his *Lohengrin* poem at the Angel Club in Dresden, where the audience, which included Robert Schumann, the painter Schnorr von Carolsfeld and the architect Gottfried Semper, was distinctly impressed. But a discussion ensued between Wagner and a doctor named Franck as to whether this romantic poem should have a tragic ending or not. For some time Wagner himself vacillated. Frau von Lüttichau was the first to set his doubts at rest, assuring him that the opera could only end as it did, tragically. Wagner abandoned all alternative endings: after all, a woman, whether called Elsa or Minna, who put the forbidden question and refused to accept the incomprehensible as an established fact was her own executioner. 'Lohengrin was looking for a woman who would believe in him without asking who he was or whence he came, one who would love him as he was and because he was what he seemed to himself to be. He was looking for a woman to whom he need not justify himself . . .'

Once again it is the world of myth that fascinates Wagner without, however, completely detaching him from history. During work on *Lohengrin* he was thinking of an opera about Siegfried and a play about Barbarossa. But historical figures are not adaptable, they cannot have autobiographical features grafted on to them, whereas with myths, which, as Wagner always emphasized, are of popular origin, poetic licence is permissible. Wagner's latent enthusiasm for the

Franz Liszt conducting

Wagner, after a
watercolour of 1853

classics was fanned by his discovery that the saga of Zeus and Semele contained the embryo of the *Lohengrin* myth. It would not be long before he was envisaging the *Art-Work of the Future* in Hellas.

On his flight from Dresden Wagner took with him practically all his most recent works. As far back as the late summer of 1848 he had been dipping into the *Nibelung* saga for the first time and had also 'amused himself' with Titurel and Parsifal while busy on *Lohengrin* and *Tannhäuser*. He was also acquainted with Hans Sachs, who was to liberate him from *Lohengrin*. Tristan alone was still not even a name. For a while Wagner also considered a drama (without music) entitled *Jesus of Nazareth* in which Christ should appear as the bringer of social-revolutionary ideas. The plan was discussed with Bakunin and shortly afterwards dropped.

It looks as if Wagner needed an incubation period for all his manifold plans. At any rate, from 28 April 1848, the day he finished the score of *Lohengrin*, till the autumn of 1853, when he began work on the *Ring* music *(Rheingold)*, he produced only sketches of the music; the libretto, however, was completed by the end of 1852.

On 28 August 1850, Liszt conducted a performance of *Lohengrin* at the Weimar Court Theatre. Wagner's detailed written instructions as to the technical requirements afford an astonishing insight into his sureness of touch as a producer, even though he makes impossible demands on the theatrical amenities of the time.

Art-philosophy   The day of Wagner the philosopher was now at hand. His first treatise was called *Art and Revolution* (1849), while the second was devoted to the *Art-*

Stage designs by Wagner himself
for the first performance of
Lohengrin in Weimar

Entwurf zu:

Wiland der Schmied.

Heldenoper in drei akten.

Personen.

Wiland der Schmied.
Eigel der Schütz. } brüder.
Helfrich der Arzt
Schwanhilde.

Neiding, König der Niaren.
Gram, sein marschal.
Der böte Rothers von Schweden.
Bathilde, Neidings tochter.

Erster akt.

nach Norweg: waldiger uferraum am meere. im vordergrunde, zur seite, Wiland's haus mit der schmiede, welche frei davon steht. – Wiland feilt und schmiedet an einem

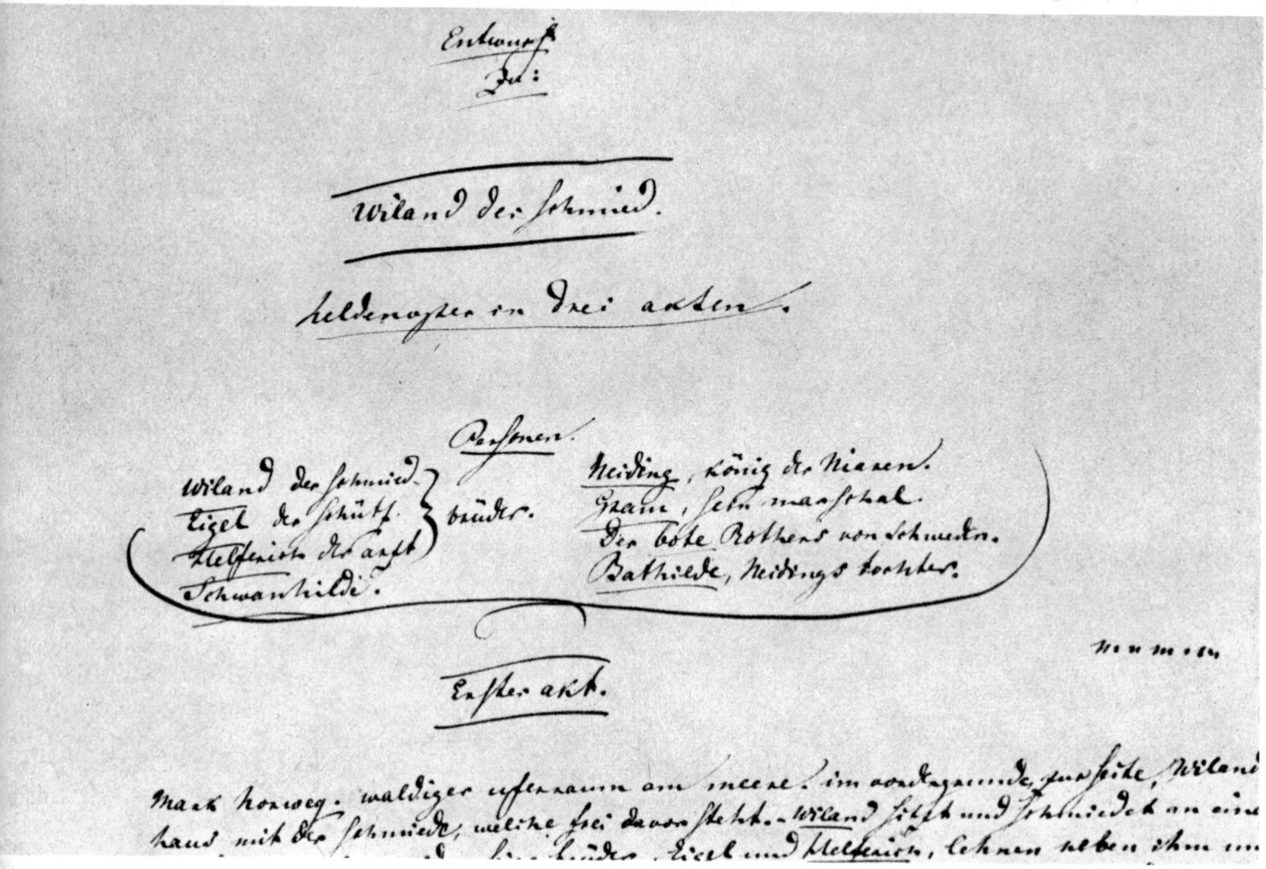

Sketch for *Wieland the Smith*

Work of the Future. This in turn led to the prose sketches for a 'heroic opera' in three acts called *Wieland the Smith*; once again the scene is set vividly: 'When Neiding's retinue break into the house to take Wieland the Smith the whole smithy caves in with a terrific crash and only the side walls are left standing. A holocaust on all sides. Above the pall of smoke Wieland hovers in the air with outstretched wings.'

And so to Zürich, where there were domestic as well as artistic crises to be faced. Minna, arriving from Dresden with the dog and parrot, had lost faith in Richard. It was he who had jeopardized even her modest standards by writing controversial pamphlets she could not understand instead of an opera that would appeal to the public. Now it was she who pressed him to go to Paris – and his destiny.

A young English girl named Jessie Taylor had attended the first performance of *Tannhäuser* in Dresden with her friends the Ritters. Three years later, now Jessie Laussot, a bride of nineteen, she visited Wagner with Karl Ritter, full of homage and admiration. Hearing in Bordeaux that Wagner was in difficulties she now turned over to him a substantial sum of money, backed by her wealthy mother and Frau Ritter. Wagner regarded her as his 'angel', and as his new Paris plans were making no headway he visited her at Bordeaux. She listened enraptured to his aspirations and, like Wieland's bride Swanhilde, fell more and more under his spell. One day Minna received a letter from Wagner, suggesting that they should henceforth live apart. Minna deployed all her resources to keep her husband and eventually succeeded when Jessie (of whom no portrait exists) declined to follow Wagner blindly to the Middle East. And Minna was there to receive her contrite husband on his return home.

About eighteen months later, in February 1852, Wagner met Otto Wesendonck and his wife Mathilde. At first they were just casual acquaintances, for there were still reverberations of the Jessie episode, with Eugène Laussot, the

The former *Aktientheater* in Zürich

wine merchant, playing the part of the jealous Hunding and the former Swan-hilde now cast as Sieglinde. After the libretto of *Rheingold*, dated 31 March 1852, came *Walküre*, Wagner having decided in October 1851 to expand *Siegfried's Death* into a tetralogy. The idea of linking *Siegfried* with some kind of Festival had first occurred to him a year previously, on 14 September 1850.

It was not till the summer of 1853 that Wagner began to see the Wesendoncks again. On 29 May he composed a *Polka* for Mathilde and sent it round to her with a note: 'something to melt yesterday's ice.' And by 19 June she was being presented with a *Sonata* and a note asking 'how will it be, do you think?' Mathilde Wesendonck was far from being what Wagner imagined her. She was naturally flattered by the gushing, if unrequited, protestations of a man who, after all, was one of Zürich's celebrities. She had literary ambitions and later wrote a tragedy called *Edith, or the battle of Hastings* as well as some dramatic

Otto Wesendonck

Mathilde Wesendonck

scenes glorifying Frederick the Great. All her life she needed some intellectual focus outside her domestic life: her first was Wagner; then she tried unsuccessfully to attract Schopenhauer; and finally attempted to interest Wagner's direct opposite, Johannes Brahms, in composing music for some ceremonial verses of hers for use at cremations.

Minna Wagner, a watercolour of 1853

For Wagner, Mathilde was nothing more than an echo: she substantiated him without making any positive contribution of her own. It may well have gone to her head to see how much she meant to an artist of Wagner's stature, but when it came to the point she failed him. She must have incurred Minna's antipathy the evening she decried Minna's favourite *Rienzi* and extolled the later works. Minna viewed the growing understanding between Richard and Mithilde with mistrust. She was under no illusions about her own position; at the age of forty a return to the stage was out of the question, while a separation would reduce her to anonymity. Skilfully mustering all her feminine resources she even succeeded in rekindling Wagner's physical passion, for during a journey in Switzerland, far from carrying out his intention of running away from her, he implored her to join him. In his letters she is 'dear little kitten' and 'good old Minna' as well as the 'hasty, unfair, suspicious, in short, bad wife': and he signs himself 'roast marmot gobbler', 'old parson', 'your dear old man' or 'your ridiculously faithful husband'.

But this was only one of the conflicting currents by which he was tossed: the other was driving him toward the point of no return with Mathilde. Otto Wesendonck, a wealthy silk-merchant and art-lover, generous and well-bred, offered the Wagners a small house in the grounds of his magnificent mansion. Mathilde called it 'a real haven *(Asyl)* of peace and friendship'. No need now for any more of those formal visits: Wagner had long made a habit of calling on Mathilde every afternoon between five and six and playing her the passages of

The Wesendonck villa near Zürich

The *Album-Sonata*
for Mathilde Wesendonck

The 'Asyl' in the grounds of the Wesendonck villa

Walküre he had composed that morning. She called him her 'dusk man', and he wrote at the foot of the sketch of the *Walküre* prelude the letters G. S. M.: '*Gesegnet sei Mathilde*', blessed be Mathilde.

The 'Asyl'   At the 'Asyl' Wagner worked on *Siegfried* and was visited by old friends such as Eduard Devrient and Tichatschek as well as by Hans von Bülow and his young wife Cosima, *née* Liszt. Sitting together round the Wesendonck table one evening in 1857 were Minna, Mathilde and Cosima...

Wagner had first discovered Schopenhauer in 1854 and was by now well versed in his philosophy. He understood *The World as Will and Idea,* but it had much less influence on his thinking than is generally supposed. What Wagner found in Schopenhauer was merely the confirmation of his own ideas. Just as he preconceived the world of Freud, so he had already divined the world of Schopenhauer; for Wagner, the philosopher was not a prophet but a second copy of himself. Though they never met, Schopenhauer let Wagner know that he ought to give up music as he had far greater talent as a writer. And as for himself, he, Schopenhauer, proposed to stick to Mozart and Rossini.

Yet it was neither the Schopenhauer nor the Wesendonck chapters that brought Wagner to *Tristan.* It was simply the wish, understandable in view of the huge scope of the *Ring*, to 'write a practicable Opus that would bring in something and keep my head above water for a while'. He even toyed with the idea of having *Tristan* translated into Italian for the Emperor Pedro of Brazil, who wanted a Wagner opera for Rio de Janeiro, but after some preliminary discussions the plan came to nothing.

Arthur Schopenhauer

It was Calderon, not Schopenhauer, who provided the intellectual stimulus for the new work, the opening theme of which was scrawled on the edge of the score of *Siegfried*. Nor was it Wagner's intention to feel himself as Tristan and exalt Mathilde to the stature of Isolde. He had glimpsed the world of *Tristan* long before it became reality. For him, what ensued was what he called 'the greatest miracle': 'the preconceived, substantial Something was finally manifested to the poet himself.' Mathilde presumed she herself was the model for Isolde, but Wagner termed her '*Frau Calderon*'. For a brief moment of eternity Mathilde threw herself into Wagner's arms when he handed her the poem of *Tristan* as soon as he had finished it. At this moment Wagner imagined that his beloved would consecrate herself to death that he might live. Instead of projecting his love-life into the closing scene of *Tristan* he projected *Isoldes Liebestod* into his own world, and even he was incapable of immediately distinguishing between wish and reality.

The world of Tristan

Minna and Mathilde

The sequel was like a tragi-comedy. The score of *Tristan*, into which Wagner inserted some of his settings of Mathilde's poems, progressed steadily. Then one day, Minna intercepted a letter from Wagner to Mathilde and unable to comprehend it deduced an *affaire*. Her behaviour made it impossible for Otto Wesendonck to continue the arrangement he had made for his wife's sake, confident of her love. Yet for a while there was yet another period of calm. The ailing Minna went off to do a whey-cure, but her behaviour on her return made any continuation of the existing *ménage* impossible. At a pinch she might have tolerated a young rival, but Mathilde's intellectual and social superiority was something she could not and would not accept. And so to the final rupture: on 17 August 1858 Minna wrote to Mathilde, starting: 'Before I depart, I want just to say as my heart bleeds that you have succeeded in taking my husband away from me after nearly twenty-two years of married life. I hope this noble achievement will be a comfort to you and make you happy'.

Wagner shed no tears on leaving the 'Asyl'. His last visitors were Hans and Cosima von Bülow, and the former was also present as chaperon when Wagner bade farewell to Mathilde.

First stay in Venice

It was on 29 August 1858 that Wagner set eyes for the first time on the city where he was to die: Venice. He rented quarters in the Palazzo Giustiniani and fitted them out with a profusion of dark red hangings, curtains and carpets. In the middle of a vast room stood the piano which was to bring *Tristan* to life.

Wagner was unaccompanied, but his thoughts were with two women, with Mathilde, for whom he started a diary, and with Minna, to whom he wrote a number of moving and affectionate letters. Once again the two currents were at work. His 'dearest pet' was told what her husband was doing, what he was eating, and how marvellous the Austrian military bands were, playing his music on the Piazza San Marco. Minna wanted to make him a rug to put under the

The fair copy of the *Tristan* score

The Palazzo Giustiniani in Venice

piano: her 'good little husband' begs her to send it forthwith: 'it will be so lovely to finish the last act of *Tristan* on *your* rug.' Two days previously he had written in the diary he was keeping for Mathilde: 'Your caresses are the crown of my life, the blissful roses that flower out of the crown of thorns that is my head's only adornment.'

Back in Paris   In April he saw Mathilde again, and he was often at the Wesendoncks' before going on to Paris. But the familiar 'Du' had now become the formal 'Sie': the dream had faded into something like disenchantment.

On 17 November 1859 Minna arrived in Paris, and once again she and Richard set up house together.

The idea of trying his luck in Paris a third time came from Liszt; so here was Wagner back again in the city where in 1840 he had been in a debtors' prison. His circumstances were still far from promising. True, he was known now, if only for his pamphlets, too well known in fact. His pleas and requests fell on deaf ears and it was only a word from Princess Pauline Metternich, the wife of the Austrian Ambassador, to the Emperor Napoleon III that enabled Wagner to stage *Tannhäuser*. For months he had to combat a phantom he himself had conjured up eleven years previously when he temporarily abandoned music for pamphleteering.

Of all Wagner's many dreams, the *Art-Work of the Future* was the one that had the most serious consequences. From a single word written in 1850 a whole ideology was deduced. Only once had Wagner explicitly used the expression '*Gesamtkunstwerk der Zukunft*'. It was not long before he was hoping never to hear the words again, and he even to some extent gave the lie to them. But for his interpreters it sufficed that the words had been used.

Princess Pauline Metternich

The 'Gesamtkunstwerk' was what Herder had been hoping for, as well as for 'someone to overturn the whole collection of rags and tatters masquerading as opera and erect an Odeon, a temple where Poetry, Music, Action and Scenery are all gathered together under one roof'.

Wagner on the other hand, with his eyes on classical antiquity, spoke of the kinship of music, poetry and dancing; only thus, in his view, could drama result. As regards scenery he contradicted himself. In his *Art-Work of the Future* he spoke of an 'appropriate background' of architecture and landscape painting, and of an 'environment of physical Nature' for the dramatic artist. In a letter to Ludwig II, however, he relegates scenery to the level of 'a silent, contributory background': music, words and action are definitely more important than scenery. 'Look less and listen more' was how he put it. The notorious 'Gesamtkunstwerk', the synthesis of all the arts, existed for him only in the verisimilitude of the whole.

Wagner's contemporaries were bound to regard the *Art-Work of the Future* as a challenge, especially Meyerbeer, for whom opera had always been a world

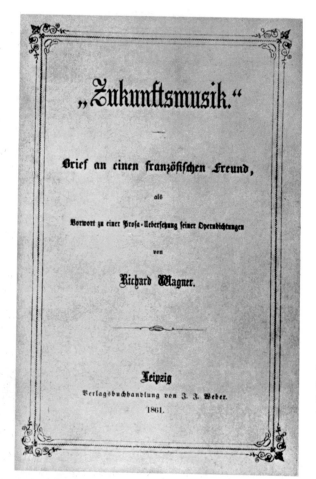

Title page of an open letter intended as the 'Preface to a prose translation of his opera libretti'

A caricature of 1869:
'Wagner punctures the ear-drums
of his audience'

of make-believe. The entire artistic world rose against it. Singers, with some justification, saw a danger to their 'harangue', their hallowed practice of turning every scene into one long *aria*. And as if on a secret signal all the papers suddenly came out with caricatures representing Wagner's theories as an attack on the ear-drum, although Berlioz, in his *Requiem* for instance, used a far larger orchestra than Wagner ever did. However, it was Wagner who was given the honorary title of 'musician of the future'.

His counter-attacks only made matters worse. The musicians were only too glad to have a chance to defend themselves against this trouble-maker who cynically derided all that they held most sacred – and most convenient. Yet it may well be that although Wagner's artistic theories were provocative enough, and his preoccupation with German legends was rejected, especially in Latin countries, an appreciable factor in the steadily mounting opposition to him was something quite different, namely the aggressive pamphlet *Judaism in Music* which he had published in 1850 under the pseudonym of K. Freigedank. When Wagner began dictating his life to Cosima in 1865 he admitted that nearly all the troubles that beset him in his best years stemmed from this pamphlet. Wagner's friends and enemies put their own interpretations, which were seldom identical, on the *Art-Work of the Future* and *Judaism in Music*. The pamphlets made him only enemies, instead of money.

For Wagner, Paris was anything but a Promised Land. 'After all, it is terribly unpatriotic to want a comfortable life in the main lair of the enemy of the German people. Good Germans should really do something to relieve the most German of all opera composers from this fearful ordeal.' This was just another of those egregious pronouncements of Wagner's with a deal of bitterness in them, not against the French but against his fellow-Germans, for whom he was still a political renegade. He had no illusions as to his position in Paris. 'I do not believe that a French version of my opera will be any good, and everything I do to promote it is against an inner voice that I can only stifle by force or frivolity. Nor are my endeavours being blessed by Fortune.'

Tannhäuser
in Paris

There were one hundred and sixty-four rehearsals for *Tannhäuser*. Since there was no possibility of the performance being given in German the work was translated into French by Charles Truinet, and all the singers were French except the Tannhäuser, Albert Niemann. The conductor was a certain Dietz, whom von Bülow called 'a senile old dolt without intelligence, memory or ear'.

The management had new costumes and scenery made, and in all a quarter of a million francs are said to have been lavished on the preparations for the first night. Wagner added a Bacchanale to the first act, an opera without a ballet being unheard of in Paris; but he categorically refused to pander to the Parisian habit of including a ballet in the second act as well. The dancers, robbed of their traditional interlude, mobilised their Jockey Club friends . . .

Not even the presence of the Emperor could avert the pandemonium. At the second performance Niemann lost control of himself in the third act, and when his Narration was also greeted with derision and booing he flung his pilgrim's

Tannhäuser poster in Paris

Paris: Albert Niemann as Tannhäuser

hat into the audience in a fit of rage, only pulling himself together to bow to the royal box, where he had noticed the Emperor and Princess Metternich demonstratively applauding.

After the third performance, which was also systematically sabotaged, Wagner withdrew the score. The only reward for eighteen months of toil was 750 francs in royalties.

Yet it was the *Tannhäuser* fiasco of 13 March 1861 that made Wagner popular in France. He won over Auber, Gounod and Saint-Saëns, and Baudelaire also took Wagner's part in a pamphlet: 'What will Europe think of us Frenchmen, and what will Germany say about Paris? This handful of nit-wits is bringing us all into disrepute.'

Now that he was free to travel anywhere in Germany except in Saxony, where he was still not amnestied, Wagner went to Weimar for a musical festival and then on to Karlsruhe to discuss the first performance of *Tristan*. Nothing doing. But he was hopeful of finding adequate soloists in Vienna, where on 11 May 1861 he heard *Lohengrin* for the first time, first the dress rehearsal and then the première, at which he was accorded an extraordinary ovation. So *Tristan* was promised to Vienna instead of Karlsruhe.

Corrections to the *Meistersinger* poem in Wagner's own hand

Original manuscript of the Meistersinger poem

Never was Wagner so much on the move as during these months. It was the manifestation of an inner unrest, his relations with Minna constituting more and more of a problem. He went to Venice with the Wesendoncks, 'finding them very happy together', which made him feel even more lonely. He had met Cosima von Bülow again at Bad Reichenhall and been given 'an almost timid look of enquiry'. His base was still Paris, where in a small room in the Hôtel Voltaire the first version of the *Meistersinger* poem began to take shape. The idea of a light-hearted opera had suddenly come to him in Venice during a mood of abject depression, and the figure of Hans Sachs, which had first introduced itself in July 1845, was beckoning again. During his return from Venice to Vienna, after bidding Mathilde farewell ... 'now at last I am completely resigned', 'helplessly enmeshed between the past and the present', the whole of the *Meistersinger Overture* came into his head 'with the utmost clarity' even before the poem was finished.

The firm of Schott at Mainz was interested in the new work and paid him an advance on it. The first orchestral sketches were made at the nearby town of Biberich just after another rupture with Minna, who had come to help him settle into a new house. One day she intercepted a harmless letter from Mathilde, and this was the beginning of 'ten days of hell'. Eventually Minna went back to Dresden, after Wagner had attempted to allay her fears for the future, not however without adding categorically: 'If each of us henceforth looks after his own happiness and welfare it will be best for both of us.' The letter ends: 'Heartfelt thanks and sincere greetings from your Meistersinger.'

Before it had got beyond the proof stage Wagner was already making important alterations to the 'Prize Song'. Minna, as well as Mathilde, was kept informed as to how well the now work was progressing, and so was another Mathilde, a lawyer's daughter of twenty-nine whom Wagner had met at the Schotts' in Mainz. She had made him some sugar-coated biscuits in the shape of the *Lohengrin* swan. Mathilde Maier remained a true friend of Wagner's right up to the 'Wahnfried' days: she seemed to personify the figure of Eva, 'child and woman'. She was a Germanic beauty, clever and very well read. Later, Nietzsche kept up a correspondence with her. It was her youth and femininity that attracted Wagner. For the first time in his life it seemed to be a profound, almost fatherly love: what he saw in her was not so much Mathilde as Minna when she was young. It was not sexual desire, but appreciation of her quiet, almost motherly ways that led him to implore her to come to Vienna and run his house for him. 'I need the feminine element, someone who is resolved, in my present lamentable circumstances, to be to me all that a woman can and must be if I am ever to enjoy life again.'

Mathilde Maier

Mathilde could not take the plunge; she remained the 'good friend', platonic. She died, almost stone deaf, in 1910.

Wagner's confidante for many years,
Mathilde Maier

The Frankfurt actress
Friederike Meyer

Once again the two currents are flowing in opposite directions. At about this time Wagner began to go about with a Frankfurt actress named Friederike Meyer, a sister of Luise Dustmann who was ear-marked for Isolde in Vienna. A protegée of the Intendent of the Frankfurt opera, she gave up her engagement for Wagner's sake and accompanied him to Vienna, where tongues soon began to wag. It was her own sister who observed that the impecunious Wagner was obviously skinning her, a remark that can be taken in two ways. But when the *affaire* began to jeopardise the performance of *Tristan* Wagner packed her off to Venice and never set eyes on her again.

The villa at Penzing, Vienna

There followed the most incredible part of Wagner's life, the heady delights of sudden success. Concerts in Vienna led to a tour of Russia which brought in a substantial sum. He at once rented a villa in the Viennese suburb of Penzing and fitted it out on a most luxurious scale, as if to blind himself to the fact that though he was now fifty he still did not amount to anything in society. It was decorated to his own lavish specifications: 'the walls were festooned with silk, and a light hanging from the ceiling cast a dim radiance. The whole of the floor was covered by heavy and uncommonly soft carpets into which one's feet literally sank.' The working-room was lilac, with lilac hangings and bands of dark red and gold in the corners. The dining-room pattern was rosebuds. The curtains were of brown wool with a Persian pattern, and the arm-chairs were of dark red plush. The maid had to wear pink knee-breeches and be exquisitely perfumed...

To pay for all this was obviously impossible, and in March 1864 Wagner vanished into the blue to evade his creditors. 'Unless a miracle happens, this is the end.'

Sketch of the apartment at Penzing, with Wagner's detailed instructions about the decorations

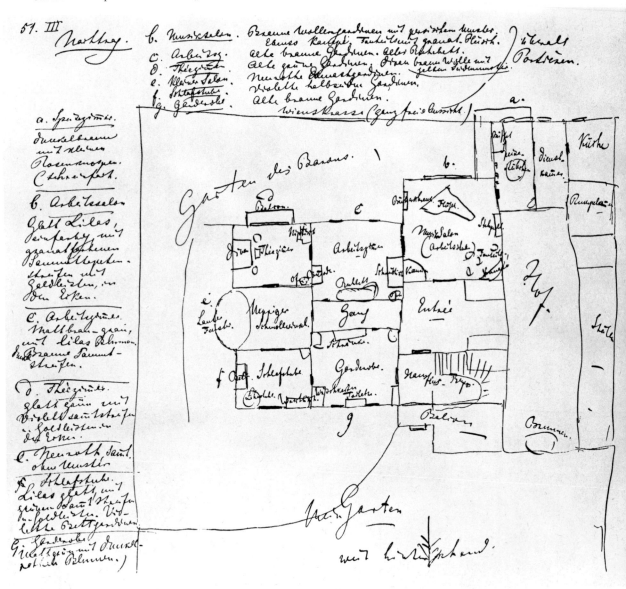

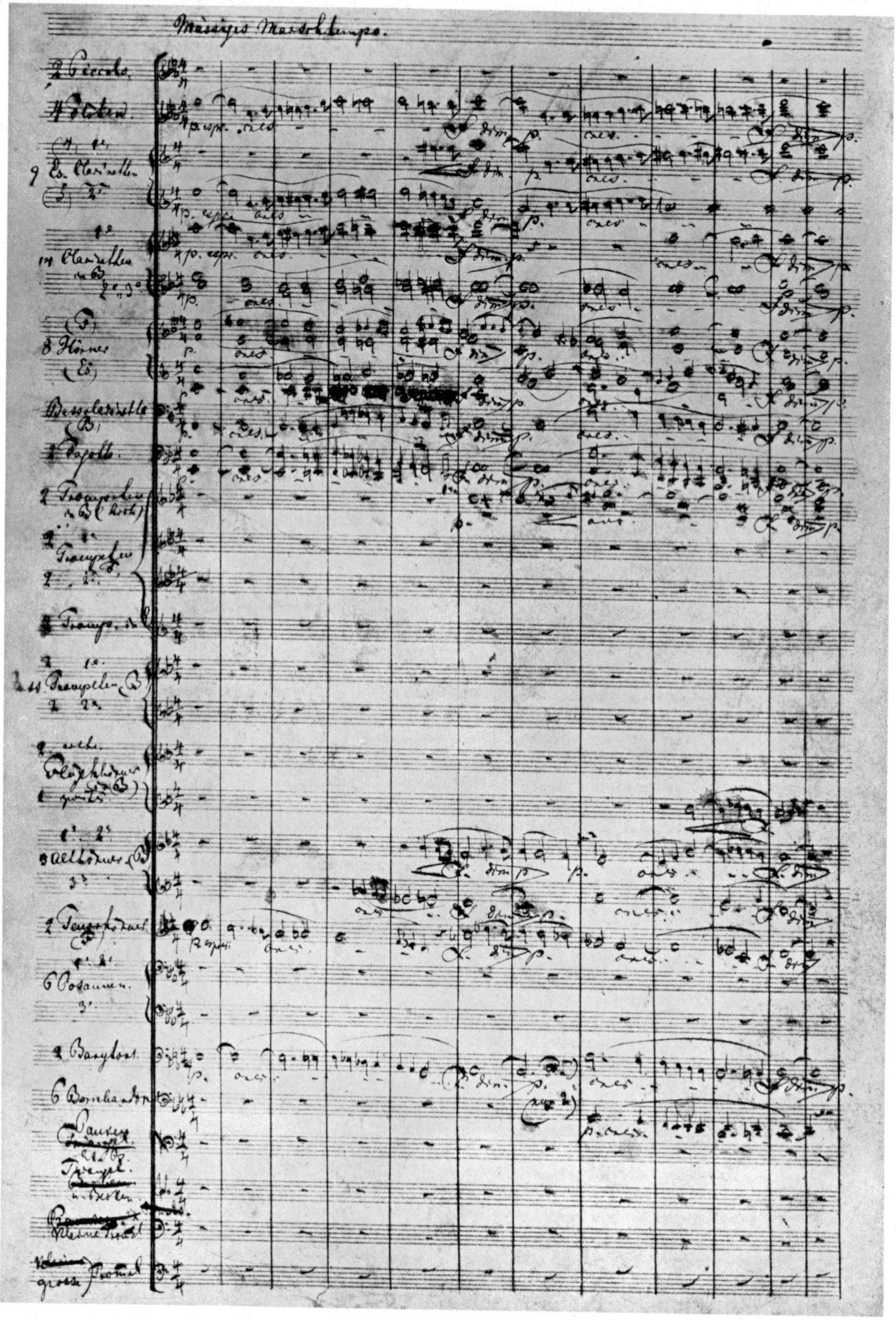
Mässiges Marschtempo.

The *Huldigungsmarsch* (Homage March)
for Ludwig II

King Ludwig II of Bavaria

The miracle did happen. On 3 May 1864 Wagner was astonished at being waited on in his Stuttgart hotel by the Secretary of King Ludwig II of Bavaria, *Hofrat* Franz Seraph von Pfistermeister, with a summons to Wagner to present himself at the Munich Court forthwith. Next day Wagner, fifty-one, and the young King, barely nineteen, confronted one another for the first time. Ludwig had read the *Art-Work of the Future* at the age of twelve and attended a performance of *Lohengrin* at sixteen. So when he came upon the question, in the foreword to the text of the *Ring*, whether the work would ever enjoy the patronage of some princely Maecenas, Ludwig immediately heeded the call.

Ludwig II

Mathilde Maier was one of the first to be told of the miracle:'and lo, a wondrous youth, sent by Destiny to be my saviour!'... 'Our encounter yesterday was one long love-scene without end. He has the most profound comprehension of my nature and my needs. He offers me everything I can possibly want for my life and work, and for performances of what I have written.'

The young King gave Wagner 4,000, and then another 16,000 gulden to clear his Vienna debts. 'How do I feel after all this? As if I were no longer alive, but dead and in Heaven.' 'And all this now, at the very darkest, nigh unto death hour of my existence.'

Richard Wagner
at the age of fifty-two

Model of the projected Festival Theatre in Munich

They met almost every day, and each saw in the other his own God. Rapt in their dreams they mused and planned: the *Ring* was to be completed and Gottfried Semper was to design a special Festival Theatre for it looking down over Munich from the banks of the river Isar. The fee for the *Ring* was to be 30,000 gulden payable in advance. The *Flying Dutchman* was to be performed, and *Tristan* too, which had been abandoned in Vienna after seventy-seven rehearsals. Wagner became the King's most trusty confidant and put his thoughts on paper for him: *On State and Religion* and *On a German Music School to be Founded in Munich*. Many of the thoughts were the same as those he had tried fifteen years before to bring to the notice of the King of Saxony.

Opposition was immediate. Both the Catholic clergy and the Court were afraid that the unstable King would succumb completely to this Protestant 'northerner'. Within a year came the first Press attack on Wagner.

Parsival.

Anfortas, der Hüter des Grales, siecht an einer unheilbaren Speerwunde, die er in einem geheimnissvollen Liebesabenteuer empfangen. Titurel, der ursprüngliche Gewinner des Grales, sein Vater, hat im höchsten Alter dem Sohne sein Amt, somit die Herrschaft über die Gralsburg Monsalvat, übergeben. Er muss dem Amte vorstehen, trotzdem er sich durch den begangenen Fehltritt dessen unwürdig fühlt, bis ein Würdigerer erscheint, es ihm abzunehmen. — Wer wird dieser Würdigere sein? Woher wird es kommen? Woran wird man ihn erkennen? — —

Der heilige Gral ist die krystallene Trinkschale, aus welcher einst der Heiland beim letzten Abendmahle trank mit seinen Jüngern zu trinken reichte. Joseph von Arimathia fing in ihr das Blut auf, welches aus der Speerwunde des Erlösers am Kreuze herabfloss. Sie ward als heiliges Heiligthum lange Zeit der sündigen Welt geheimnissvoll entrückt. Als in rauhester, feindseliger Zeit, endlich unter der Bedrängniss durch die kriegerischen Ungläubigen, die heilige Noth der Christen [...] am höchsten stieg, stieg die Sehnsucht, das [...]

The prose sketch of *Parsifal*

Sketch for a Buddhist drama *Die Sieger*

Çakya-Muni. Ananda. Prakriti. (deren Vater u. Mutter.) Brahmanen. Junger. Vater. —

— Der Buddha auf seiner letzten Wanderung. — Ananda am Brunnen von Prakriti, dem Tschandala-mädchen, getränkt. Heftige Liebe dieser zu Ananda; dieser erschüttert. —

Prakriti, in heftigsten Liebesleiden: ihre Mutter lockt Ananda herbei. Grosser Leidenschaftsausbruch: Ananda bis zu Thränen ergriffen, und gerührt ohne [...] von Çakya erlöst. —

Prakriti [...] der Ur-Buddha, am Stadtthore unter d. Baume, um von ihm Vereinigung mit Ananda zu erbitten. Dieser fragt sie, ob sie die Bedingungen dieser Vereinigung erfüllen wolle? [...] von Prakriti auf eine Vereinigung von Leben ihres Herzens [...] gedacht; sie sinkt erschüttert und schluchzend zu Boden, als sie endlich Kräfte [...] auch Ananda's Gelübde der Keuschheit ertragen. Ananda von Brahmanen verfolgt. Vorwürfe wegen der Bekassung Buddha's —

Wagner's house in Munich:
facing the garden

Wagner at once asked the King for a vote of confidence, to which Ludwig replied, 'Stay, stay here'. New plans were concocted: *Parsifal,* and *Die Sieger,* a Buddhist drama part of which had been sketched in 1856 during work on the first part of the *Ring* in Zürich, were to be the culmination of Wagner's work. His country house 'Pellet' at Kempfenhausen was not far from Schloss Berg where the King lived; nor was his Munich villa in the Briennerstrasse far from the Residenz.

Contrary to general opinion, Wagner avoided politics with the King, to the fury of those who would have been glad to make use of him. A few days before the first Press attack two emissaries from the Prince of Taxis came to see him with an offer of free shares in a new bank to be established under Jesuit auspices if he would intervene with the King to replace *Hofrat* Pfistermeister by *Staatsrat* Klindworth, a distant relative of the pianist Karl Klindworth. Prince Maximilian of Thurn and Taxis was planning to set up for his eldest son a Kingdom of Rhineland-Westphalia, which would include a considerable slice of Belgium. Jesuit circles wanted to ensure the exclusion of Prussia from Western Germany, and the proposed bank was to influence the elections accordingly. Wagner wrote to Mathilde Maier: 'The Jesuits wanted to give me two Festival Theatres, two art schools, villas and allowances, anything I wanted: all I had to do was place myself at their disposal.' When Wagner proved impervious to the most generous offers – 'by doing so I betrayed my artistic ideals' – the opposition mounted a concerted attack.

But Wagner's thoughts were with the first performance of *Tristan und Isolde*. He was its real mentor, even though the posters gave 'Herr Siegel' as the producer. The name of the conductor, in accordance with Bavarian custom, was not given, but it was Hans von Bülow.

Hans von Bülow

Von Bülow had attended the first performance of *Rienzi* at the age of twelve. The volume of sound unleashed by Wagner in the first two acts had left the sensitive boy literally deaf to the third act: he could see, but heard nothing till Act Four. This very first evening he succumbed to Wagner. Leaving home at seventeen without even saying goodbye he went to him and through the intervention of Karl Ritter showed him his compositions. Liszt accepted him as a pupil and brought out his phenomenal gifts as a pianist. Grandiose plans in the composition line were confided to Wagner, and in 1851 he seemed to be toying

After a *Tristan* rehearsal: Wagner escorts Cosima while Hans von Bülow follows with the music

Hans von Bülow

with the idea of a *Tristan* symphony or overture. 'You may have second thoughts about *Tristan*,' wrote Wagner, three years before starting on it himself. Bülow arranged excerpts from *Lohengrin* and was deputed to prepare piano scores of *Rheingold*, *Walküre* and *Tristan*. He became the *alter ego*, serving Wagner with the devotion of a Kurwenal.

In 1857, at the age of twenty-seven, he married the daughter of his teacher, and a pupil of his own, Cosima Liszt, who was barely out of her teens. The honeymoon included a visit to Wagner at Zürich, but Wagner and Cosima had already met four years earlier in Paris.

Cosima

On 21 November 1863 Wagner was still staying with the Wesendoncks in Zürich. The next day he went to Berlin and on 28 November went for a walk in the Zoo with Cosima. Then and there they sealed their troth 'thenceforth to belong to each other alone'.

There were no bourgeois repressions about Cosima, daughter of the Countess d'Agoult, and no pricks of conscience concerning her retiring, complex-ridden husband. When von Bülow was summoned to Munich by Wagner, who

Scene from the first performance of *Tristan und Isolde*, 1865

had manipulated his appointment as Court Kapellmeister, Cosima and the two children Daniela and Blandine came too. Nine months later, on the day of the first orchestra rehearsal for *Tristan*, Cosima presented her husband with a third daughter, Wagner's. She was christened Isolde. Bülow had no suspicions: he was preparing *Tristan*, which he had previously gone through under Wagner's supervision, for the projected performance at Karlsruhe. He also played to the King: Beethoven, Liszt, and of course Wagner. A macabre set-up: the ailing King hidden behind a screen, and Bülow playing away for hours on the piano while Wagner is with Cosima, 'who is a law unto herself'.

Almost a hundred years after the first performance: *Tristan* at Bayreuth

It was on 10 June 1865 that that haunting, enigmatic *Tristan* chord was heard for the first time. In Ludwig and Malwina Schnorr von Carolsfeld, husband and wife, Wagner was sure he had found the ideal pair, Ludwig in particular coming up to his highest expectations. After four performances they both went back to Dresden, and shortly afterwards Ludwig died of typhoid. Wagner and Bülow arrived too late for the funeral and returned at once to Munich without visiting Minna, whom Richard had not seen since November 1862. Their correspondence was mainly devoted to financial matters, but there was nearly always a message for the parrot.

Theurer Freund!

Bleiben Sie, bleiben Sie hier,
Alles wird herrlich wie zuvor.
Ich bin beschäftigt. — Lieb' in den Tod!

Ihr
Ludwig.

11 März 1865.

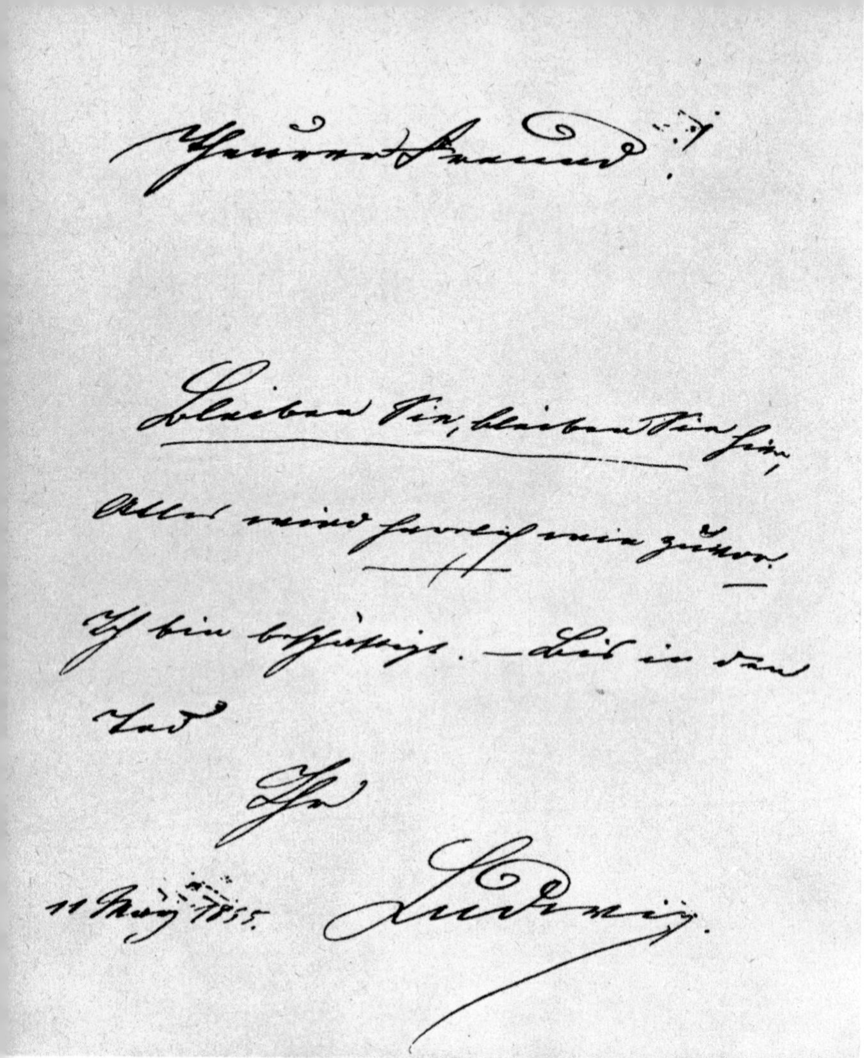

Ludwig II orders Wagner: 'Stay here!'

The first performance of *Tristan* brought the King and Wagner even closer together. The infatuated monarch wanted to know everything about his 'beloved friend', so on 17 July 1865 Wagner began dictating his autobiography *Mein Leben* to Cosima. Shortly afterwards he also began chronicling his thoughts for the King's benefit, but only kept it up for fourteen days. It almost looks as if Wagner had already begun to have doubts about his royal friend, who had sworn to be unswervingly faithful unto death yet often did the very opposite of what he had agreed upon with Wagner. Though they began to see less of each other, they still corresponded frequently; Wagner in a bare twenty years

A chalk drawing of Wagner
by Franz Lenbach

wrote two hundred and fifty-eight letters, forty poems and seventy telegrams, and the King one hundred and eighty-three letters, three poems and eighty-six telegrams. Nearly all of them are in the same effusive tone of their first over-emotional encounter. Wagner, who as early as October 1865 was finding this 'royal love' 'a veritable martyr's crown', was constantly inventing new forms of fulsome adulation, well aware that the King, on whom his fortunes depended, expected them.

But he also soon realized that Ludwig II was, in fact, not really capable of understanding either his musical or his philosophical ideas.

'Triebschen'

In December 1865, yielding to pressure from his Cabinet and his family, the King asked Wagner to leave Munich: 'After all, it is not for ever.' Wagner complied, having been given another 40,000 gulden a few weeks previously. He almost seemed to welcome the new development. 'My dear child, it was inevitable. One day driving with the King in a coach and four, and the next set upon by the Papists, when all the time all I wanted was to get on with my work in peace; it was too ridiculous,' he wrote to Mathilde Maier from Vevey. So while Cosima, 'like Noah's dove', kept in with the King by making him a cushion embroidered with the 'symbols of all those sublime works', the Dutchman's ship, Tannhäuser's staff, Tristan's cup and Siegfried's sword, Wagner after a break of two and a half years resumed work on *Die Meistersinger* at a country house near Geneva.

Wagner's next port of call was Marseilles, where he received a telegram from Dresden saying that Minna had died suddenly on 25 January. So now he was free.

'Triebschen'　　In March 1866 Cosima arrived in Geneva. Crossing Lake Lucerne one day she and Richard spotted a villa called 'Triebschen'. Wagner moved in in mid-April, the rent being paid by the King, who was 'suffering frightfully' at their separation. In May Ludwig turned up unexpectedly at 'Triebschen' *incognito* to celebrate Wagner's fifty-third birthday and had a long talk with him, more about politics than about Wagner's work. Everything pointed to war between

Prussia and Austria, Bavaria's ally. Ludwig was thinking of abdication and joining Wagner for good.

Richard's and Cosima's second child, Eva, was born at 'Triebschen' on 17 February 1867. Cosima was still married to von Bülow, and it is difficult to see what induced the three of them to keep up the pretence. It may be that Wagner was afraid of the reaction of Ludwig, who had turned a deaf ear to insinuations and remained loyal to both Richard and Cosima until he too learned the truth. Or it may be that Cosima was loath to cause either her husband or her father trouble, and even Wagner was afraid of Liszt's anger. Bülow, on the other hand, shielded both his wife and his friend as soon as he saw that Cosima was indispensable to Wagner's composing. Wagner in turn needed von Bülow, the only person he could really trust as an artist. And Bülow was definitely to conduct *Meistersinger,* which was gradually nearing completion.

Franz Liszt with his
daughter Cosima von Bülow

Wagner with his daughter Eva,
born in 1867

In March 1867, after an 'exile' of fifteen months, Wagner returned to Munich, but only for a short visit. After a brief audience with the King he was given another substantial sum, 12,000 gulden. Shortly afterwards there was a serious difference between them: Wagner had engaged for a performance of *Lohengrin* his old friend Tichatschek, whose appearance so displeased the King that behind Wagner's back he ordered the part to be sung by Heinrich Vogl, whereupon Wagner took himself off to Lucerne without even saying goodbye.

A year later Wagner enjoyed his greatest triumph with the first performance of *Die Meistersinger von Nürnberg*, Bülow conducting. Contrary to all etiquette Wagner, at Ludwig's request, watched the performance from the royal box. 'The impression made by the King's gesture was overwhelming ... Wagner, who had been branded as a heretic and exiled, ... was rehabilitated, and in no uncertain fashion.'

After the first performance
of *Die Meistersinger:*
Wagner expressing his
gratitude from the royal box

Luther (auf der Wartburg) nach furchtbaren Aufregungen, am geöffneten Fenster durch einen lauen Luftstrom, den Blick in das Grüne, den Gesang eines Vogels, – ein andermal selbst durch einen tüchtigen Zug Einbecker Bieres, schnell verwandelt, (weich gestimmt, sich erkräftigend, zu neuem „Ein' feste Burg“). — Hieran die räthselhafte Wirkung des Blickes eines weiblichen Auges; darin die Tiefe des Unwissens, kühlende Sanftmuth, Sicherheit der Beschränktheit: dies, plötzlich der in das Schrankenlose gerissenen Phantasie des streitlich bewegten Mannesherzens entgegentretend, wirkt beschämend, [illegible], unterjochend. Was? der Mann, in welchem die ganze Welt gährt, der dieses Weib mit all seinem Verstand tausendmal übersieht: ist's nicht demüthigend? Teufelsspuk? Und doch, ist's nicht mehr als jener Luftzug, jener Vogelgesang, und namentlich auch als jene Kanne Einbecker Bier? Ist's dir nicht erst erwacht, und was du doch dir selbst erst sagen musst, vermag es dir es nicht aus sich hervorzurufen zu sagen: „Bruder, [illegible] u. gedenke!!“ Und diese Hand, die dir den Trunk reicht, die Lippe die ihn segnet? – Aber die blonde Flechte Catharina's, wenn sie über die Kissen hinunterhing, wird sie dich nicht auch sich über den Arbeitstisch zu hängen? – doch! es wär' zu versuchen. — 19 Aug.

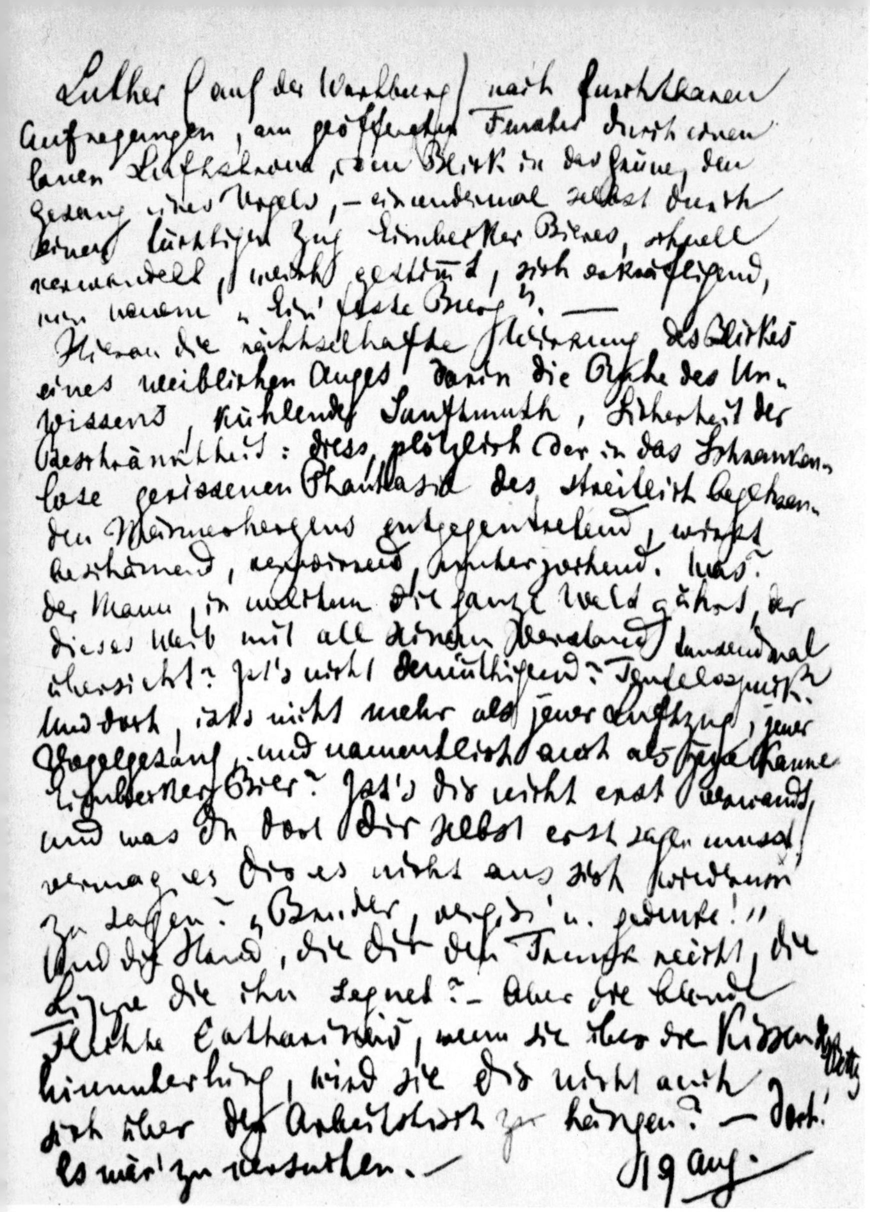

Sketch for a projected play *Luthers Hochzeit*

Although on the way home to 'Triebschen' the 'exultant Siegfried' *motif* suddenly came into his mind, Wagner was overcome by a 'complete lack of energy for any kind of movement'. Suddenly the figure of Martin Luther occurred to him, and a play, *Luthers Hochzeit,* was planned. It remained a fragment, as was nearly always the case when instead of intuitively comprehending his subject Wagner merely projected his own sensations on to an alien form. What was really concerning him was not Catharina von Bora but Cosima; a Protestant wanting to marry a Catholic wife.

At last, caught one day in a terrific thunderstorm during a walking-tour in the Alps with Richard, Cosima decided to part from her husband. Bülow declined to give his wife her freedom; Cosima left him for good, taking with her Isolde and Eva, of whom Bülow still thought he was the father. On 6 June 1869 Siegfried Wagner was born.

On 25 August 1870 Richard and Cosima were married in the Protestant Church at Lucerne. Bülow had bowed to the inevitable. From now on he served Wagner at a distance, playing for the various Wagner Societies and giving a concert for the Bayreuth Festival Fund. He never saw Wagner again, but when he heard of his death in February 1883 he completely broke down.

Cosima and Richard Wagner

Wir beehren uns, hiermit unsere am 25. August d. J. in der protestantischen Kirche zu Luzern vollzogene Trauung anzuzeigen.

Richard Wagner.

Cosima Wagner, geb. **Liszt.**

Wedding announcement, 1870

Friedrich Nietzsche,
whom Wagner met in 1868

'Triebschen' now became what the 'Asyl' could never have been, a real home where Wagner could enjoy the peace and quiet he needed for his work, with a *ménage* of six servants, two peacocks, two cats and a horse.

On Easter Monday 1869 Friedrich Nietzsche, who had been appointed to a Chair at the University of Basle, paid his first visit to 'Triebschen'. He had been introduced to Wagner, whom he hero-worshipped in his boyhood in the old Leipzig days, and had excited the latter's admiration by his exact knowledge of philosophical works. It was this visit to 'Triebschen' that ultimately bore fruit in his *Birth of Tragedy out of the spirit of Music*.

There were, however, a number of reasons for the hero-worship turning to inveterate hostility. After *Parsifal* Nietzsche maintained that Wagner had 'betrayed' their common ideals. The earlier admiration and profound understanding ended in whole-hearted vituperation, a swing that was by no means solely due to Nietzsche's mental and physical breakdown. Years after Wagner's death Cosima, whom Nietzsche regarded as 'the only woman of real class', was still receiving messages such as 'to Princess Ariadne, my beloved' from his deranged fancy. And when Nietzsche was put into an asylum he exclaimed, 'It is my wife Cosima Wagner who has brought me here'.

A new 'Kurwenal' presented himself: Hans Richter, pianist, conductor and selfless friend. Gradually he took Bülow's place, being ear-marked to conduct the *Ring* tetralogy which was nearing completion at 'Triebschen'.

Early in January 1872 a strange letter arrived from Russia: the pianist Joseph Rubinstein offered his services in the execution of the *Ring*. On the eve of Wagner's departure for Bayreuth he arrived of his own accord at 'Triebschen' and was at once taken on by Wagner, no questions asked, to copy parts, to be his 'personal pianist', and to arrange a piano score of *Parsifal*.

Hans Richter, who conducted the *Ring*
at the first Bayreuth Festival

The Rubinstein letter: 'I am a Jew'

Wagner had suggested 1867–68 to King Ludwig II for the great performance of the whole of the *Ring;* but by 1869 he had not even finished *Siegfried* and it was not until 21 November 1874 that the vast work was completed.

It was twenty-eight years since Wagner had had his first vision of *Siegfried,* in the company of Frederick Barbarossa, while working on *Lohengrin.* Two years later, in 1848, he sketched his first dramatic adaptation of the whole *The Nibelung* *Nibelung* saga, and finished his poem *Siegfried's Death* in the same year. In *myth* 1851 he intended to preface it with *Der junge Siegfried,* but by 1854 his 'head was buzzing with a bigger idea altogether, three dramas with a three-act prelude'.

The first *Ring motif* that Wagner composed was the 'Ride of the Valkyries', which he jotted down for a young musician on 23 July 1851. The actual composition of the whole was not started till November 1853 after an extraordinary experience at La Spezia: 'I sank into a sort of somnambulistic trance in which I suddenly had the feeling that I was sinking in a surging tide of water. The rush and roar of the waters soon took musical shape as the chord of E-flat major surging incessantly in broken chords which declared themselves as melodic figurations of increasing motion, yet the pure triad of E-flat never changed. I woke from my trance in terror, feeling as though the waves were now rushing high above my head. I at once recognized that the orchestral prelude to *Rhein-gold,* which I had been carrying about inside me without ever being able to fix definitely, had at last come to me.'

Leitmotif In the *Ring* Wagner made consistent use of *leitmotif,* which he describes in *Opera and Drama* thus: 'The central life-giving force of dramatic expression is the poet's verse-melody, to which is related, as a kind of foreboding, the preparatory and absolute orchestral melody, and from which proceeds as a memory the idea behind the instrumental *motif* ... Each *motif* should act as an emotional sign-post in the vast labyrinthine structure of the drama. Through them we are kept in constant touch with the profoundest secrets of the poet's message and participate at first hand in their realization.'

In the same treatise Wagner wrote of the orchestra's 'powers of utterance', which consisted in 'imparting what cannot be conveyed by speech'. He drew an analogy between his orchestra and the Chorus in classical Greek tragedy: in fact it was Aeschylus whom he had constantly in mind while working on the *Ring.* But Wagner himself hardly knew what his specific task was to be. He was not aware, to quote Thomas Mann, 'that he was charged with building his own musical cosmogony, nay his own mystical cosmos, and endowing it with profound organic life, the epic in sound of the beginning and end of the world'.

Ludwig II refused to wait till the *Ring* was complete, and in the spring of 1869 he commanded performances in Munich of *Rheingold* (on his birthday) and *Walküre.* Wagner attempted to get him to agree to at least one performance

The first performance of
Rheingold in Munich, 1869

before an invited audience: 'if however you feel that you must insist on even these performances being given before an ordinary theatre audience, it would be with the most painful regrets that I should witness such a procedure.'

But the King stubbornly insisted on his *Ring*. Wagner arrived in Munich three weeks before the première, which despite the royal command was not until 22 September, a month after the King's birthday, to try to rescue what was already beyond hope of salvation owing to inept production, miscasting and inadequate scenery. The conductor, Hans Richter, had already declined to have anything to do with such a 'scandalous performance', and even some of

the artists were rebelling. Still the King was adamant: 'these theatre people must learn to obey my orders, not Wagner's whims.' And '*Pereat* the whole lot of them.' He added that if Wagner persisted in his opposition his salary was to be withheld, and never again would a work of his be given in Munich.

There were cogent reasons for Wagner's opposition: from the very start he had not wanted the *Ring* entrusted to normal theatrical conditions. It was while he was taking a cold-water cure at Albisbrunn in November 1851 that the Festival idea had taken concrete shape: 'I'll build a Festival Theatre on the Rhine and issue invitations to a Dramatic Festival ...'

The Margraves' Opera House
at Bayreuth, then the
largest stage in Germany

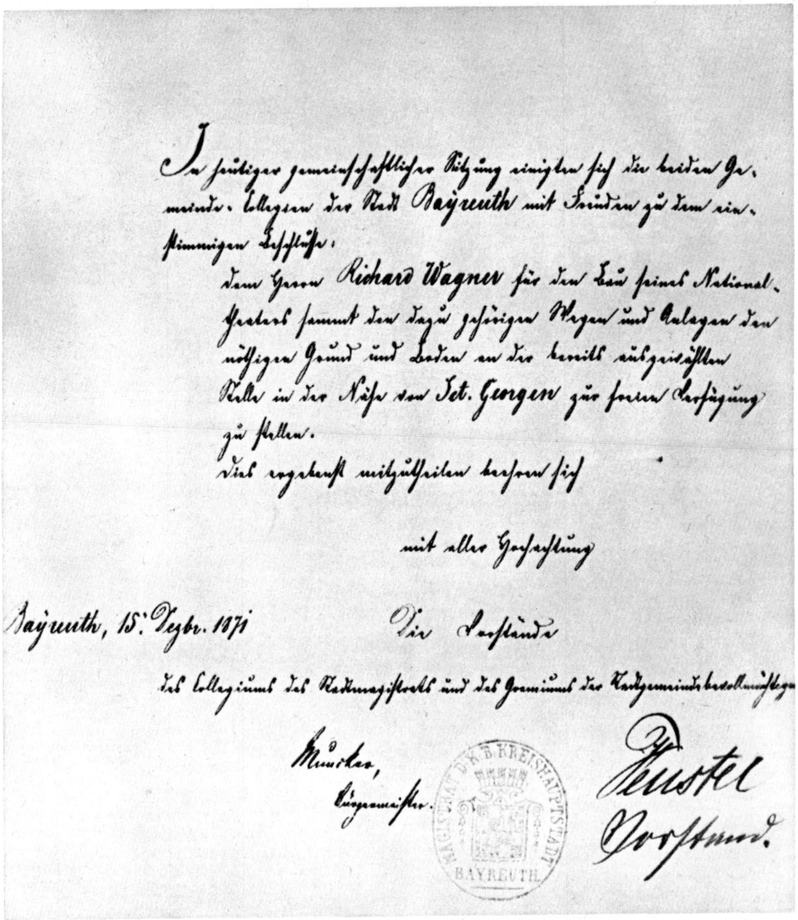

In heutiger gemeinschaftlicher Sitzung einigten sich die beiden Gemeinde-Collegien der Stadt Bayreuth mit Freuden zu dem einstimmigen Beschluße:
Dem Herrn Richard Wagner für den Bau seines National-Theaters sammt den dazu gehörigen Wegen und Anlagen den nöthigen Grund und Boden an der bereits ausgesuchten Stelle in der Nähe von St. Georgen zur freien Verfügung zu stellen.
Dies ergebenst mitzutheilen beehren sich

mit aller Hochachtung

Bayreuth, 15. Dezbr. 1871 Die Vorstände

des Collegiums des Stadtmagistrats und des Gremiums der Stadtgemeindebevollmächtigten

Muncker,
Bürgermeister.

MAGISTRAT D. K. B. KREISHAUPTSTADT BAYREUTH

Feustel
Vorstand.

The document attesting
the free conveyance
by the Municipality of Bayreuth
of a site for the Festival Theatre

Thumbing through a conversation manual at 'Triebschen' one day Wagner came upon the name 'Bayreuth'. In the 'Margraves' opera-house', built in 1747, the town boasted 'the largest stage in Germany'. This was the turning-point. In April 1871 Wagner visited the little Franconian town, which he had passed through once before on a journey from Eger (Cheb) to Nürnberg in 1835. But the theatre proved inadequate. 'So we shall have to build: so much the better.' In a New Year's letter, 1851–52, curiously tinged with despair, he had been thinking of the banks of the Mississippi, but now he was all for staging the *Ring* at Bayreuth, at the very heart of the recently proclaimed German *Reich*.

Bayreuth

From Leipzig, his birthplace, Wagner announced in May 1871 his project of producing the *Ring* in the summer of 1873 at a Festival Theatre to be built at Bayreuth. He had already made friends there, and offers of theatres in Darmstadt, Baden-Baden, Bad Reichenhall, Berlin, London and Chicago were turned down. 'Bayreuth or nowhere!' The town placed a site at his entire disposal, and when the site he had originally envisaged turned out to be unavailable, it was decided to build the Festival Theatre on the 'green hill overlooking the red Main'. On 22 May 1872, his fifty-ninth birthday, Wagner himself laid the foundation-stone.

In his choice of site Wagner showed extraordinary intuition. In the old Riga days he had experienced the remarkable effects obtainable in an amphitheatre

The Bayreuth Festival Theatre: programme of the ceremonial laying of the foundation-stone

Bayreuth: the 1876 Festival

The Bayreuth Festival Theatre:
in construction, August 1873

89

Ludwig II's declaration of patronage

The orchestra pit

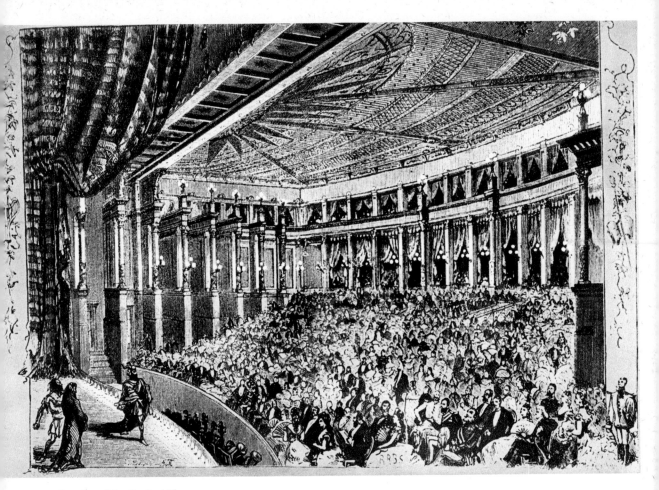

Interior of the Festival Theatre

rising in tiers. Even the idea of covering the orchestra pit originated in Riga, where the orchestra had been hidden from the public by an acoustic cover which had a wonderful effect on the orchestral sound.

The project was to be financed primarily by Patrons' Vouchers, the target being 300,000 taler, but by the end of 1874 only 300,000 marks, about one-third of the total, had been subscribed. Up to the opening of the Festival Wagner produced out of his own pocket 127,000 marks, including 20,000 marks which he had been paid for his *America March* (1876). King Ludwig II headed the list of subscriptions with a credit of 300,000 marks, which has been amply repaid by Wagner and his heirs. The King remembered his former oath: 'Help must be given, our plan must not be allowed to founder. "Parcival" is conscious of his mission and will raise all he can. Do not weaken!'

The prelude to *Rheingold* was heard for the first time on 13 August 1876 in the presence of Kaiser Wilhelm I and the Emperor Pedro II of Brazil. The exalted personages took no offence at the hastily improvised aspect of the theatre, but neither did they anything to help. In 1872 Wagner had stated that 'with this building we are only outlining an idea and presenting it to the nation to make of it a worthy monument'. But the German nation showed no particular interest in Bayreuth. 'There it stands, a fool's caprice,' fumed Wagner. The first Festival showed a deficit of 160,000 marks, part of which Wagner paid off out of the royalties that kept pouring in from all over the musical world. For the remaining 98,634.65 marks the King once again came to the rescue with a loan, to be guaranteed by the takings of the Munich Court Theatre: it was duly guaranteed.

Wagner must have found the artistic shortcomings of the Festival even more depressing. He was made hideously aware of the discrepancy between his visions and the theatrical resources of the day. He had had special equipment

A glimpse behind the scenes: the Rhine Maidens 'floating'

Bayreuth 1876: the Rhine Maidens

installed to help the Rhine Maidens with their 'swimming', but the desired effect was obstinately elusive. The chief trouble was the lighting: the producer, Wagner, had to work by gaslight from jets along the footlights and above the proscenium curtains, the amount of light on the actual stage being woefully inadequate, despite the help of the best stage-technicians of the day. The scenery was built by the leading experts available and Wagner himself supervised everything down to the minutest detail, but the shortcomings became increasingly apparent with every rehearsal. Cosima even complained that the Nordic gods looked like Red Indian chiefs. It was obviously impossible to work out a new technique of stage-design to match the new technique of music-drama, one of the chief obstacles being the detailed instructions of Wagner himself.

Bayreuth 1876: Franz Betz as Wotan

Bayreuth 1876: Joseph Nierung as Hunding

Bayreuth 1956:
Hans Hotter as Wotan

He had always expected that the world he showed on the stage must actually accord with the world of his dreams. When in 1860 he made 'a short trip to Antwerp to see Madame Lohengrin, *née* Elsa', he was bitterly disappointed to find that the site and appearance of the castle were totally different from what he had expected. So now he was forced to adapt his mythological visions to the harsh realities of his ill-lit stage and communicate some of the 'sanctity of the desert' feeling he had experienced on the Rosegg glacier. Still nothing would go right. Wagner read all the books on the subject, had Viking helmets and shields copied, and was still not satisfied, commenting bitterly on the 'false reputation of the *Ring* performances'.

But he did succeed in getting most of the cast to understand what gestures and movements he wanted. At rehearsals he acted all the parts himself with such verve that they completely forgot his diminutive stature and Saxon accent.

As a producer Wagner was foiled by the contemporary style of painting. Ludwig Richter, and even more so Moritz Schwind, were the 'right' painters for legends and sagas, and Wagner was completely enthralled by this style. On the other hand, this led him to use all sorts of old theatre tricks: the machinery,

Bayreuth 1876: Georg Unger as Siegfried

Bayreuth 1951: Bernd Aldenhoff as Siegfried

Bayreuth 1876: the Ride of the Valkyries

for instance, that propelled the Valkyries across a fantastic wooden backcloth dated from baroque days. And in order to preserve the proper proportions the figures in winged helmets brandishing spears were schoolboys – another well-worn theatrical device. The effect on the audience was undoubted, but was it what Wagner had visualized? 'A ray of light pierces the gloom: in the background the Valkyries riding, with vanquished warriors across their saddles.' He had not managed to make the costumiers see that they were dealing with 'figures belonging to a cultural epoch dissociated from experience or from anything to do with experience'. What he was offered was 'the sort of thing illustrated weeklies go in for'. He began to lose heart: 'I can't use all this stuff, and have to keep

Tricks of the theatre

Bayreuth 1957: Brünnhilde's awakening

Bayreuth 1876: Brünnhilde's awakening

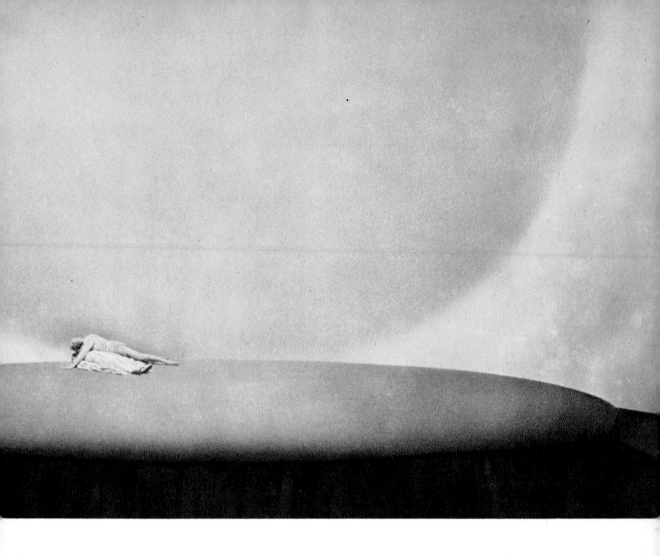

worrying about where I am to turn for help.' Later, when he was working on *Parsifal,* he envisaged Kundry as a sort of 'Titian Venus', instead of which she was swathed in impossible draperies not unlike the Rhine Maidens. He had long ago abandoned his brief dream of a *'Gesamtkunstwerk'*, and as long ago as *Tristan* had castigated purely decorative effects as 'scenic nonsense'. Now, in bitter, ironical earnest, he could only exclaim: 'How I abhor all these costumes and paint! And when I think of all those characters like Kundry being painted up, it reminds me of those ghastly artists' revels! Now that I have made the orchestra invisible, I should like to invent an invisible stage.'

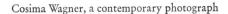
Cosima Wagner, a contemporary photograph

Cosima's power over Wagner horrified all their friends. A single glance from her sufficed to transport him to the seventh heaven of love, or plunge him into despair. 'Everything was tacit and secret: my faith in her belonging entirely to me amounted to such a degree of confidence that in my eccentric excitement I sometimes indulged in extravagant exuberance.' In the early days of their acquaintance he had once invited the young Cosima von Bülow to get into an empty wheelbarrow and said that he would wheel her back to her hotel. But when Cosima jumped at the idea, Wagner was so surprised that he could not summon up the courage to go through with the quaint escapade!

Her friends called Cosima 'the Delphic oracle'. Not that they derived much wisdom from her: all they knew was that Wagner was 'wholly and unconditionally' under her thumb. In Cosima he had found what, without admitting it, he had always been looking for, a Senta who believed in him implicitly, an Elsa who never asked him about his past or his origin, an Elisabeth who in defiance of convention protected him, and an Isolde who was prepared to die a *Liebestod* with him. Cosima was of the aristocracy in a double sense: through her the door was open to Wagner into a world in which up till then he had been at best a welcome intruder.

Cosima was also a frequent mediator between Wagner and Ludwig II, and it was she to whom Ludwig first confided his abdication plans. For many years Cosima kept the King in the dark as to the true relationship between her and Wagner.

Richard Wagner in 1877

It was not for nothing that Cosima and Richard used pseudonyms in their letters and telegrams: he was 'Will' and she was 'Vorstel'. They had read Schopenhauer together, so Wagner was the *Wille* (will) and she the *Vorstellung* (idea). This unusual but significant subterfuge was persisted in right up to the 'Triebschen' days.

From a revolutionary Wagner had changed into an absolute lord and master, so convinced of his 'mission' that he considered himself an authority on almost every subject under the sun. Now that he was so famous, now that celebrities from far and wide waited upon him, he felt like a king in the world of German art. It was not only Ludwig's munificence that had made such a difference to his finances. Performances of his early works were frequent and widespread, the most successful being *Lohengrin*, which enjoyed eighty-eight different productions during Wagner's lifetime. By 1868 it was being performed in London and

St Petersburg, in 1875 in Boston, and in 1877 in New York and Melbourne. Next came *Tannhäuser* with seventy-three different productions in Wagner's lifetime. *Rienzi*, which had been heard in 1859 in Prague and in 1864 in Stockholm, was given at a further fifty-one theatres as well, *Der fliegende Holländer* at forty-six and *Die Meistersinger* at thirty-two. But *Tristan und Isolde*, which was expected to bring in 'bags of gold', was only put on at seven theatres, as was *Siegfried*. *Die Walküre* was given fourteen different productions, *Rheingold* ten, and *Götterdämmerung* nine.

'Wahnfried'

'Wahnfried', on the other hand, the new home, was almost entirely due to royal munificence, Ludwig presenting Wagner with 25,000 taler. By the end of 1867 the Royal Bavarian Treasury had paid out to Wagner a total of 131,173 gulden and 46 kreuzer in salary, rent payments, advances and gifts. The bust of Ludwig II by the front door of 'Wahnfried' is a symbol of a royal friendship without parallel.

'Here where my illusion found peace be this house named by me "Peace from Illusion" *(Wahnfried)*.' The inscription was added after the house was finished, Wagner taking the unusual name 'Wahnfried' from a small village not far from

The 'Halle'

The 'Saal'

'Wahnfried' where Wagner settled in 1874

Cosima's lilac salon

A family portrait: Cosima,
Richard and Siegfried Wagner

Steinway Hall' in which his own music competed on equal terms with Wagner,
Verdi and Schubert.

Cosima rustled about in long, trailing dresses, and Wagner would now and
then put on his *Meistersinger* costume. The reason for his predilection for
dressing-gowns and loose, soft garments was a cogent and unromantic one: all
his life he feared a recurrence of the shingles that first attacked him in his Zürich
days.

Once again the two currents were at work: on the one hand Wagner angrily asking himself what sort of person he was, what he amounted to in the world, living in a palatial house where the servants had to address even six-year-old Siegfried as 'Sir'; on the other hand regularly patronizing the Angermann Inn like any other local citizen, drinking his beer and arguing with artists or the local worthies. It is almost as if he wanted now and then to get away from the 'Wahnfried' world, a world he had fashioned himself but in which Cosima dwelt.

With Minna jokes had been rife: the idea of calling himself anything so frivolous as 'Pimperlekef' to Cosima was unthinkable; the games in which he indulged at home, especially with the children, were probably little to her liking. It was Cosima who supervised their upbringing, and once when they were all getting ready for a journey to Vienna she insisted on 'prominence' being given to the Habsburgs in their history lessons so that the children 'should show even more interest in the ruling house of Austria as soon as we set foot on Austrian soil'.

Wagner in the Angermann Inn at Bayreuth

Apotheosis

1876–77: caricatures of Wagner in
German, English and Austrian papers

Wagner and Court Opera Director Dingelstedt

Wagner and the opera singer Materna

Wagner composing

Wagner gets all the unwanted drums in the Austrian Ministry of War

Wagner and the head of the firm of Schott

Versailles 21 Februar 1871

Hochverehrter Herr

Ich danke Ihnen, daß Sie dem deutschen Heere ein Gedicht gewidmet, und daß Sie mir dasselbe haben übersenden lassen. So sehr ich mich geehrt fühle, daß Sie dieses vaterländische Gedicht, wie mir gesagt wird, für mich allein bestimmen, so sehr würde ich mich freuen es veröffentlicht zu sehen.

Auch Ihre Werke, denen ich von jeher meine leb-hafte, wenn auch zuweilen mit Neigung zur Opposition gemischter Antheil zugewandt habe, haben nach harten Kämpfen den Widerstand der Ge-[illegible] überwunden, und ich glaube und wünsche, daß denselben noch viele Siege, [illegible] und [illegible] beschieden sein werden.

Genehmigen Sie die Versicherung meiner ausgezeichneten Hochachtung

v Bismarck

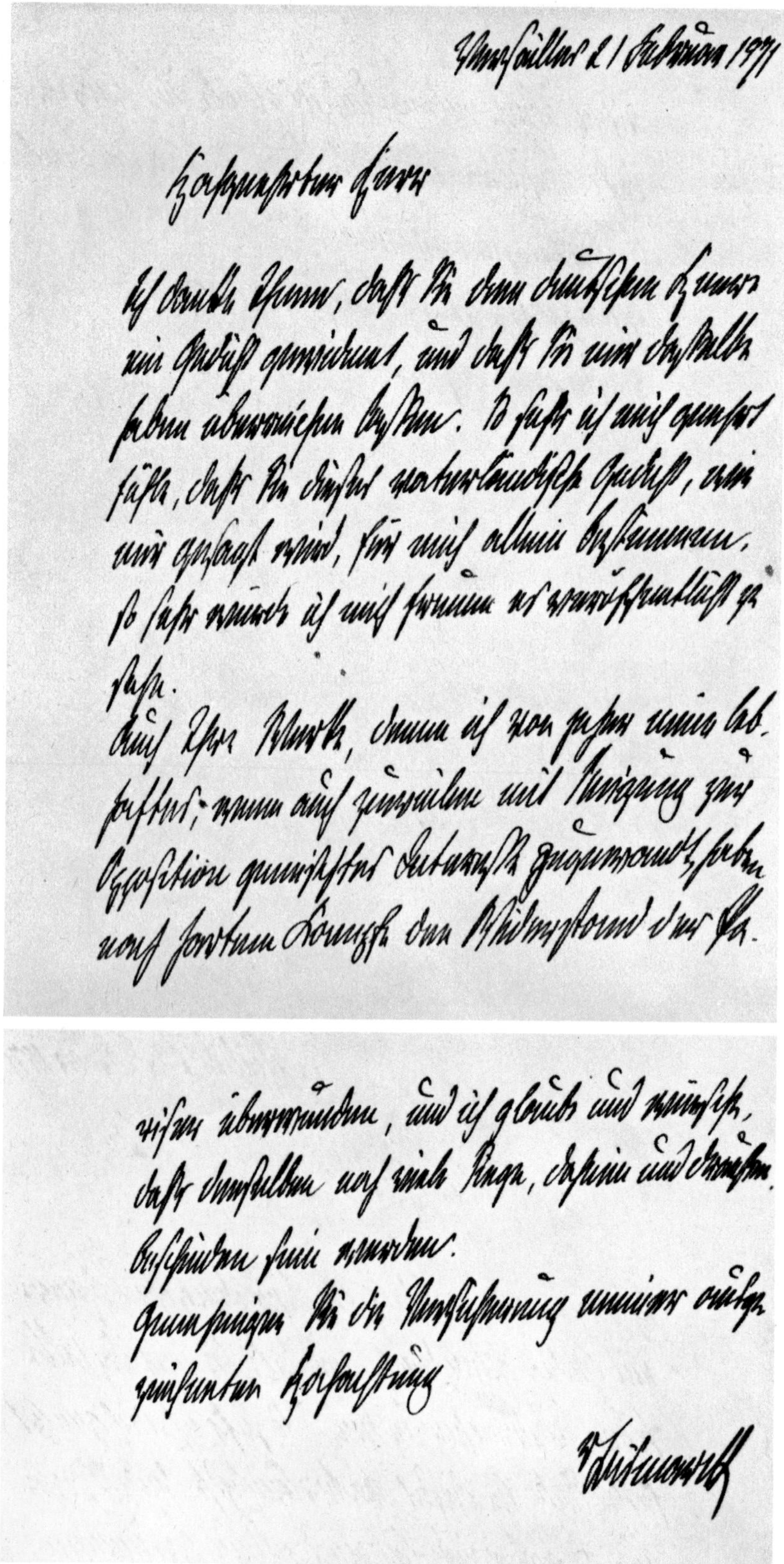

Bismarck's answer to Wagner's poem *To the German army at the gates of Paris*

The *Romeo and Juliet* theme

Wagner too probably talked politics now and again at the Angermann. There was plenty to talk about: Bismarck had created the *Reich*, with Bavarian help. As recently as 1866 Bismarck had been for Wagner 'a bad copy of the most un-German character'; later he came more and more under Bismarck's spell, possibly seeing in him a future patron of Bayreuth. He identified him with the whole idea of the *Reich* as interpreted by Konstantin Frantz, a publicist who asked Wagner for 'a clarion-call to the entire German nation, to wake it from its slumber'. Wagner's response in 1871, before leaving 'Triebschen', was a *Kaisermarsch* incorporating the old Lutheran chorale 'Ein' feste Burg' with a fanfare-like *motif*.

Towards the end of January 1871 Bismarck was handed at Versailles a poem by Wagner entitled *To the German army at the gates of Paris*. Wagner was still entertaining the idea of writing a symphony 'For the fallen', to include a theme he had jotted down in his 'brown book' in May 1868, when he was working on *Die Meistersinger*, entitled *Romeo and Juliet*.

All these plans, including a 'Hymn to greet our returning soldiers', came to nothing. A 'Comedy in classical style' entitled *Die Kapitulation* was also abandoned: Wagner attributed his authorship to 'Aristop Hanes'. The piece was only indirectly concerned with the events of 1870, Wagner satirising the capitulation of the Germans to the Paris opera and operetta in some really atrocious doggerel.

This unfinished comedy, for which incidentally Hans Richter was invited by Wagner to compose the music, was only one of several curiosities Wagner was busying himself with at this time: there were also a 'Motto for the German Fire-brigade', a 'Child's catechism' (a question and answer game on the name 'Cosima'), the 'Grand Festival March for the opening of the celebrations in commemoration of the centenary of the United States', and an anti-vivisection tract, to name only a few.

Pamphlets   At 'Wahnfried' he also started writing musical treatises again, such as *On actors and singers,* a commentary on Beethoven's Ninth Symphony, and a 'final report on the circumstances and fates that attended the execution of the Festival Play *Der Ring des Nibelungen* up to the publication of its text'.

The *Ring* afforded – and still does – plenty of scope for humour. Most of the derision was directed at Wagner's use of medieval alliterative verse and of words invented by himself. His critics failed to grasp that alliterative and onomatopoeic phrases like '*Weia, Waga, woge zur Welle*' were deliberately coined as a sort of mystic utterance largely compounded of old German expressions. In Wagner's view, the figures of the Nibelung saga could not be made to speak the language of ordinary mortals. The composer of music had also to be a composer of words, putting together a verbal score, as it were, out of rhythms and chains of consonants.

The numerous caricatures in the entire European press, and the articles ridiculing Bayreuth as the idea of a crank hurt Wagner less than the lack of interest shown by the German nation. He had hoped that Bismarck, whom he had met in 1871, would do something for Bayreuth, and he also counted on the support of Kaiser Wilhelm I and the German Reichstag; but for no obvious reason all his hopes

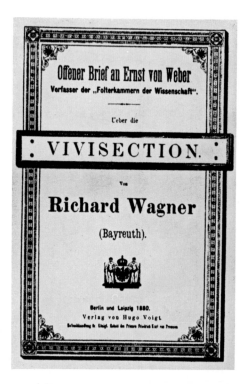

Curiosities: the anti-vivisection tract

were disappointed. The faithful few made up for a lot, but not for everything. Wagner had believed in a German nation, but when he made subscriptions available to the general public through a circular sent to four thousand bookshops the response was precisely six taler contributed by Göttingen students. 'I find the world in general and Germania in particular increasingly odious . . .'

It was a young French girl who charmed Wagner out of his depression, Judith Gautier, the daughter of Théophile Gautier. Her friends called her 'the hurricane'. She was a wild and passionate creature: Cosima described her as a 'gamine with a Roman profile'. Like a good many other young people in France Judith found Wagner's music intoxicating and lost no time in seeking his acquaintance. After a short correspondence she and her husband Catulle Mendès duly arrived at 'Triebschen' and were soon on friendly terms with Richard and Cosima. Richard, now fifty-nine, was bowled over by Judith, aged twenty-one. He executed daring climbs to show how youthful he was – until there came a timely warning from Cosima.

Judith Gautier

Cosima carried on a correspondence with Judith and gave her a lovely sunshade, but Richard put Catulle's back up by giving rein to his old love-hate for France. It was *Die Kapitulation* that led Catulle to make the final break: 'though I am no longer his friend, as I used to be, I am still a fervent disciple.' In 1873 he and Judith were divorced and Judith came alone to Bayreuth for the *Ring*. She became Wagner's 'abundance', 'the overflowing cup of my intoxication'. He avowed that 'in those days, which brought disappointment to so many and left me so unsatisfied, you were the only ray of hope. You were imbued with an infinitely sweet, soothing and yet intoxicating fire. Would that I could kiss you just once again, my dear one, my sweet!'

Judith Gautier

Bernhard Schnappauf, the barber, Wagner's factotum, was pressed into the rôle of postman, and a number of Judith's letters to Richard (she was still corresponding with Cosima) were entrusted to him for delivery. Only Wagner's letters have survived, a touching blend of ardent love and practical commissions. Would Judith please do some shopping for him in Paris, a divan coverlet, for instance, which he would like to call 'Judith', and all sorts of exquisite and exotic perfumes and powders and cold creams? 'Be extravagant, especially with

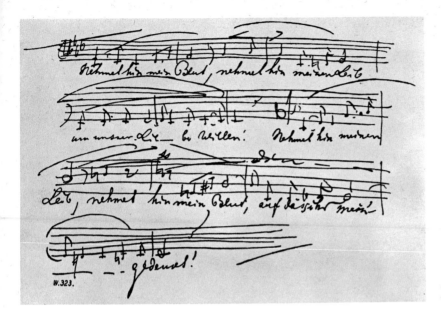

For Judith:
the *Parsifal* theme

Working on the production of
Parsifal (from left to right):
Paul von Joukowsky, décor;
Hermann Levi, conductor;
Karl Brandt, stage-manager

Bayreuth 1882:
Parsifal and the Flower Maidens

Final page
of the score of *Parsifal*

Bayreuth 1882:
Thérèse Malten as Kundry

Bayreuth 1882: the temple of the Graal

the bath-salts: the bathroom is just under the room where I compose and I like to savour a fragrant aroma issuing from it ... Everything is so tragic, everything that is real! A thousand kisses, R.'

Parsifal   A 'fragrant aroma' for *Parsifal*, another of the ideas that first came to him in Marienbad in 1845 simultaneously with *Lohengrin* and *Die Meistersinger*. During work on *Tristan* the figure of Parsifal beckoned to him again: to the languishing Tristan, Parsifal was to appear like a messenger from another world. It was then that the first draft of the poem took shape. In 1865 Wagner considerably extended its scope for King Ludwig II but did not start on the music till 1877, after the first Bayreuth Festival. He also altered the spelling from 'Parzifal': 'The name is Arabic, the old troubadours did not understand it. "Parsi" – think of the parsees who invoke fire – means "pure", and "fal" means

Bayreuth 1951: the temple the Graal

"foolish".' So Wagner to Judith, but the future oriental expert was not convinced, so Wagner's next letter admitted that 'the Arabic dialect in which "fal" means "fool" or "bumpkin" was an invention of my own ...'

This 'Christian work' was to be conducted by Hermann Levi, the son of a rabbi, and the piano score was entrusted to Joseph Rubinstein. No sooner was the choice of Levi made known than protests came in from a number of 'Wagnerians'. Levi offered to stand down, but Wagner took no notice: his only

Wagner's last abode:
the Palazzo Vendramin in Venice

The Wagners lived in the Palazzo Vendramin-Calergi on the Grand Canal. Here he wrote some articles presumably intended for a publication which he and his followers were planning entitled *Bayreuther Blätter*. All sorts of

Franz Liszt

visitors called, a particular welcome being reserved for Liszt, who stayed a week. The old differences were quite forgotten now. At the great banquet at the end of the first Bayreuth Festival in 1876 Wagner, his sparse locks crowned with a silver laurel-wreath, had gone up to Liszt: 'This is the man to whom the highest honour is due. At a time when I was quite unknown it was he who reposed the fullest confidence in me. Without him, you would probably never have heard a single note from my pen. What I have and what I am I owe to him alone, to my dear, unwavering and wonderful friend Franz Liszt.' And he embraced the aged *abbé*.

The King's last letter

In November 1882 there was a final letter from Ludwig II in answer to one from Wagner telling the King of his grief at the death of Count Gobineau. Cosima composed an 'In memoriam', a copy of which was also sent to Ludwig. Wagner opened his letter with 'Most gracious Lord and King, my heaven-sent benefactor and friend', and ended 'with his wife and children, ineffably honoured by your heavenly favour, yours for ever Richard **Wagner**, the creature of your graciousness, prostrates himself at your feet in godliness and reverence'. He had frequently admitted to Cosima that he found these letters to Ludwig 'an awful bore', yet he never departed from the rhapsodic style of address that he had first given vent to at that fateful first meeting with the King. He was well aware that the fiction must be maintained at all costs, for Ludwig still regarded Wagner as his 'dearest, infinitely beloved and esteemed friend'. The last lines of the King's letter were: 'With the most sincere love and the most steadfast faith; and may your sublime radiance shine out like the sun to give light and life to this world of ours for many a long year yet, your most faithful friend and fervent admirer Ludwig.' And of Wagner's: 'So once again may this day of my life come full circle with an appreciation of the graciousness with which I am privileged to be favoured as yours always, master and friend.' The letter was in response to Ludwig's request that Wagner should let him have *Parsifal* for private performances in Munich. But Wagner had already reserved his 'farewell to the world' for Bayreuth. After staying away from the first performance Ludwig later rode roughshod over Wagner's wishes, just as he had with *Rheingold* and *Walküre*. In the darkened royal box he had the performance in the Munich *Hof und Nationaltheater* all to himself: nobody was to be allowed to enjoy the smallest share in his property.

Memories of the *Tristan* days and Mathilde Wesendonck may well have stirred again in Venice. Wagner had seen the Wesendoncks, who had moved to Dresden, at the Festival. Otto Wesendonck had long ago got over his pique at Wagner's wish to have the

Richard and Cosima in front of the Palazzo

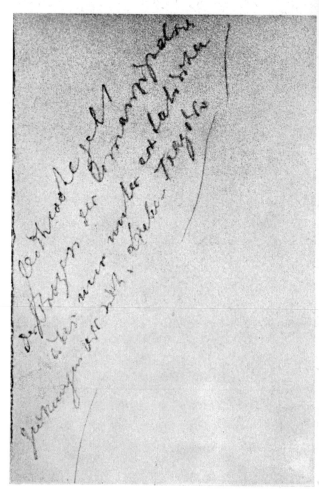

The evening before his death

The last lines before the pen slips from his grasp

Rheingold score which he had been promised and had paid for in advance presented instead to the King. A letter in the King's own hand was probably rather less gratifying to him than Wagner's avowal that 'the loving care I lavished on the musical delineation of Pogner was like setting up a monument to a friend'.

On 12 February, while Wagner was reading excerpts from Fouqué's *Undine* to the family and one or two friends, Cosima edged her diary over to Paul von Joukowsky, who had been responsible for the décor of *Parsifal,* and the painter captured Wagner's expression in a few deft strokes. Then Wagner, inspired by the nymph Undine, played the final song of the Rhine Maidens, *'Traulich und treu ist's nur in der Tiefe'*.

Next morning Wagner was at work on an article on 'The female element in human nature' and asked not to be disturbed. In an ante-room was Betty Bürckel, who though Cosima's maid actually spent most of her time looking after Richard. It was she who found him, deathly pale, his features distorted, in the final convulsions. Cosima clasped him to her, and he died in her arms on 13 February 1883 at about half-past three in the afternoon. The doctor, Dr Keppler, gave cardiac paralysis as the cause of death.

Wagner's death

The sofa on which he died

Arrival of the cortège
in Munich

The programme of the funeral

Programm

für das

Leichenbegängniß Richard Wagner's.

Vorbemerkung.

Die öffentliche Leichenfeier findet nur auf dem Platze vor dem Bahnhofe statt. Bei der Ankunft des Zuges vor der Villa „Wahnfried" wird der Sarg abgenommen und von den hiezu speziell Geladenen zur Gruft begleitet werden.

Diese Anordnung ist sowohl durch die Rücksicht auf den besorgnißerregenden Gesundheits-Zustand von Frau Cosima Wagner, als auch durch die Beschränktheit des Raumes geboten.

Um 4 Uhr wird die Leiche vor die aufgeschlagene Tribüne unter den Klängen des Siegfried-Trauermarsches gebracht.

Der Bürgermeister Muncker spricht im Namen der Stadt und legt am Sarge ein Zeichen der Verehrung nieder.

Diejenigen Herren, welche in eigenem Namen oder im Auftrage sprechen wollen, sind ersucht, dies nunmehr zu thun; dieselben werden sich der Ordnung wegen an eines der Verwaltungsraths-Mitglieder Bayreuths wenden.

Kränze und Liebeszeichen sind am Sarge und auf den vor demselben bereitstehenden Wagen niederzulegen.

Zum Schlusse wird das Verwaltungsrathsmitglied Feustel das Wort ergreifen. Nach der Beendigung dieser Ansprache trägt der hiesige „Liederkranz" einen Grabgesang vor. Der Zug bewegt sich sodann unter dem Geläute sämmtlicher Glocken und unter Trauermusik in folgender

Ordnung:

Abtheilung der Feuerwehr,
zwei Herolde,
Musikkorps des kgl. 7. Infanterie-Regimentes,
Kranzträger,
Wagen mit Kränzen,
Leichenwagen,
Geistlichkeit,
die Vertreter Seiner Majestät des Königs von Bayern
mit dem Sohne des Verewigten,
die nächsten Freunde des Hauses,
Deputationen und Künstler,
die Vertreter der Presse,
das kgl. Offizierskorps,
die kgl. Civilbeamten,
das Musikkorps des kgl. 6. Chevaulegers-Regiments,
die musikalischen Vereine der Stadt Bayreuth,
die Gemeindevertretung,
die Bürgerschaft.

Bayreuth, 18. Februar 1882.

Der Stadt-Magistrat.

Muncker.

The funeral procession at Bayreuth

Cosima wished only to die too: she had sworn never to abandon him, not even in death. As if turned to stone she sat with the body all night. A sculptor named Benvenuti made a death-mask, and then the body, with the old black silk coat and the student's cap, was laid in a bronze coffin. Just as it was being nailed down Cosima placed a cushion on Richard's chest; it was stuffed with her long hair, which she had cut off with her own hand.

On her instructions all the decorations in his room were torn down, and all the hangings, coats, cushions and roses burned. His study at 'Wahnfried' was also dismantled.

On 16 February the cortège of gondolas set out, the leading gondola bearing wreaths from King Ludwig II and King Umberto, the latter brought by Garibaldi. Among the pall-bearers was Gabriele d'Annunzio. Passing the Palazzo Giustiniani the gondoliers raised their oars in salute to the place where *Tristan* had taken shape.

Ludwig II shut himself up in Neuschwanstein on hearing the news. 'The artist whom the world mourns was discovered by me: it was I who rescued him for the world.'

Cosima did not attend the funeral at Bayreuth. It was Siegfried, walking behind the coffin, who had to calm the dogs howling for their dead master. At Wagner's wish there was no inscription on the gravestone: the world would know whose grave it was.

The death-mask

Eighty years after his death, discussion of Wagner and his works has still not abated. During his lifetime he turned the musical world upside down, besides being by far the most controversial composer of his age. To some he was the greatest genius of the nineteenth century, to others a bombastic ranter. The curse that his critical and philosophical writings brought down on his head is still not entirely expiated. There have been harsh, malicious words spoken by Stravinsky and Milhaud: there have been words of veneration and esteem from Arthur Honegger and Carl Orff.

Today perhaps we can take a more detached, more sharply focussed and less prejudiced view than the Wagnerians and anti-Wagnerians of his own day. It was not until our own time that *Tristan* was revealed as the great rupture with traditional systems of harmony, and *Parsifal* as one of the firmest foundations of the new music. Without the latter there could have been no *Pelléas et Mélisande* from Debussy, no *Elektra* from Strauss, no *Verklärte Nacht* from Schönberg.

And yet there are still a great many people who cannot dissociate Wagner's music from his showy, egocentric personality. As if human frailties and idiosyncrasies have ever been the criterion of a work of art! His detractors, after scrutinizing his controversial pamphlets, conclude that Wagner was one of the figures chiefly responsible for what came over Germany fifty years after his death, to which no less a figure than Thomas Mann could only reply, repeatedly and emphatically, that 'it is quite unjust to place a contemporary interpretation, the interpretation they would be given today, on Wagner's nationalistic gestures and pronouncements. To do so would be to calumniate and abuse them, to sully their romantic purity'.

It is his work, not his personality, on which today's admiration is centred. The spell that Bayreuth casts over the whole world is stronger than ever. The unswerving, and at times inspired, consistency of Wieland and Wolfgang Wagner has made it the home of an established tradition, living and contemporary, with nothing of the museum about it. They are both guided by the firm conviction that Richard Wagner's day, far from being done, is perhaps still to dawn.

1813 Wagner is born on 22 May, the ninth child of the police official Friedrich Wagner, who died on November 23.

1814 Wagner's mother Johanna Rosine, *née* Paetz, marries the painter and actor Ludwig Geyer on 28 August. The family moves to Dresden.

1822 Richard Wagner entered at the Kreuzschule at Dresden as Richard Geyer.

1828–30 At the Nikolai Secondary School in Leipzig.

1829 Wagner's enthusiasm is aroused by Wilhelmine Schröder-Devrient as Fidelio.

1830 Wagner attends the Thomas-Schule in Leipzig. His *Concert Overture in B-flat major* performed at the Leipzig Opera on 24 December.

1831 Wagner enrolled at Leipzig University as a music-student. In the autumn he begins lessons with Theodor Weinlig, a cantor at St Thomas's Church.

1832 Publication of *Sonata in B-flat major*, opus I, dedicated to Weinlig. Incidental music to Raupach's *König Enzio* first performed in March. *Concert Overture in D minor* and *Symphony in C major* performed at the Gewandhaus.

1833 In January Wagner completes the libretto of his opera *Die Feen* adapted from Carlo Gozzi's *La donna serpente*. His theatrical career opens with a post as chorus-master at Würzburg.

1834 Completion of the score of *Die Feen* (performed posthumously in Munich in 1888). At the end of July Wagner takes up a post as musical director of Bethmann's theatrical company at Lauchstädt, where he meets Minna Planer.

1834–36 Director of Music at Magdeburg, where his opera *Das Liebesverbot* (based on Shakespeare's *Measure for Measure*) is given for the first time on 29 March 1836, Wagner himself conducting. On 24 November 1836 he marries Minna Planer at Königsberg.

1837 Wagner takes up a post as Director of Music at Königsberg in April, and by the end of July has sketched an opera named *Rienzi* after a novel by Bulwer Lytton. In August he is appointed Director of Music at Riga. *Rule, Britannia, Overture*, first performed in 1838.

1839 In July he has to run from his creditors, and after a stay in London he arrives in Paris on 17 September.

1840 Completion of the score of *Rienzi*. Wagner becomes a contributor to the *Gazette Musicale de Paris*.

1841 Completion of the score of the *Flying Dutchman*. The short story *Eine Pilgerfahrt zu Beethoven*.

1842 Return to Germany. First performance of *Rienzi* at Dresden Court Theatre on 20 October, conductor G. Reissiger.

1843 First performance of the *Flying Dutchman* at the Dresden Court Theatre on 2 January, Wagner himself conducting. On 2 February, Wagner is appointed Kapellmeister to the Royal Court of Saxony. At Teplitz-Schönau in July he makes the first sketches for *Tannhäuser*.

1845 Completion of the score of *Tannhäuser* on 13 April. First prose sketch for *Die Meistersinger* (16 July). Completion of the prose sketch of *Lohengrin* (3 August). Première of *Tannhäuser* at Dresden on 19 October, Wagner conducting.

1846 Wagner conducts Beethoven's Ninth Symphony in the so-called Old Opera House in the Zwinger at Dresden — 'a historic undertaking'.

1848 At the Dresden 'Vaterlandsverein' reunion Wagner reads his treatise on *The relation of Republican efforts to the Monarchy*.

1849 The Dresden uprising breaks out on 30 April, Wagner taking part with words and advice, though not with arms. On 16 May a warrant is issued for his arrest. On 28 May Wagner flees to Zürich. *The Art-Work of the Future*.

1850 The Jessie Laussot episode (16 March — 3 July). Completion in August of his treatise on *Judaism in Music*. First performance of *Lohengrin* at the Weimar Court Theatre on 28 August, Liszt conducting. A letter to the painter Kietz dated 14 September contains the first hint of the Festival idea.

1851 The *Communication to my friends*.

1852 In Zürich Wagner makes the acquaintance of the Wesendoncks.

1853 At La Spezia the Prelude to *Rheingold*, which he had been struggling with for some time, suddenly comes to him on 5 September. First meeting with Cosima Liszt, then eighteen, in Paris on 10 October. Concerts in Zürich in May.

1854 Completion of the score of *Rheingold* in January. First sketches for the music of *Walküre* on 28 June. Wagner studies Schopenhauer's *The World as Will and Idea*. First conception of *Tristan* towards the end of October.

1855 Wagner conducts eight London concerts.

1856 Completion of the score of *Walküre* on 23 March. In September, the first sketches for the music of *Siegfried*.

1857 Conception and first sketches of *Parsifal* (4 April). The move into the 'Asyl', the cottage in the grounds of the Wesendoncks' villa near Zürich. Wagner starts on prose sketch of *Tristan* on 20 August.

1858 On 17 August Wagner leaves the 'Asyl' and travels to Venice without Minna.

1859 Completion on 18 March of the second act of *Tristan*. The whole score of *Tristan* completed on 6 August at Lucerne.

1860 Concerts in Paris and Brussels.

1861 The *Tannhäuser* tumult in Paris on 13 March. In Vienna, Wagner receives an enthusiastic ovation at a performance of *Lohengrin*. During a railway journey from Venice to Vienna in November the Overture to *Die Meistersinger* is composed. Work is started on the libretto of *Die Meistersinger* in Paris in December.

1862 Visits to Mainz, Biebrich, Karlsruhe, Dresden and Vienna. On his forty-ninth birthday Wagner composes the Prelude to the third act of *Die Meistersinger*: 'Wahn, Wahn, überall Wahn!' On 7 November he sees Minna for the last time.

1863 Concerts in St Petersburg, Moscow, Budapest and Prague, and in Karlsruhe, Dresden and Vienna. On a walk in Berlin, Wagner and Cosima von Bülow vow 'to belong to each other alone'.

1864 Wagner leaves Vienna to evade his creditors. At Stuttgart he receives a summons to the Court at Munich, and meets King Ludwig II of Bavaria on 4 May.

1865 10 April. Birth of Isolde, daughter of Wagner and Cosima von Bülow. First performance of *Tristan* at the Court Theatre in Munich on 10 June, Hans von Bülow conducting. First prose sketch for *Parsifal* (27—30 August). On 6 December Ludwig II is forced to instruct Wagner to leave Munich.

1866 Death of Minna in Dresden on 25 January. In March, Cosima von Bülow and Wagner discover the house at Triebschen on the Lake of Lucerne.

1867 Eva, second daughter of Wagner and Cosima, born at 'Triebschen'. Completion of *Die Meistersinger* on 24 October.

1868 First performance of *Die Meistersinger* at the Court Theatre in Munich on 21 June, Hans von Bülow conducting. At the King's wish, Wagner watches the performance from the royal box and receives a great ovation. In November Wagner meets Friedrich Nietzsche.

1869 On 6 June Siegfried, the third child of Richard and Cosima, is born. Against Wagner's wishes *Rheingold* is performed in Munich by royal command on 22 September, F. Wüllner conducting.

1870 First performance of *Walküre* in Munich, again contrary to Wagner's wishes, on 26 June, F. Wüllner conducting. On 25 August Richard and Cosima are married in Lucerne.

1871 In April Wagner travels to Bayreuth to see whether the old Opera House of the Margraves can be used as a Festival Theatre. On 12 May he makes a public announcement in Leipzig of his intention to have the *Ring* performed in 1873 in a new Festival Theatre at Bayreuth. Wagner is received by Bismarck.

1872 The foundation-stone of the Bayreuth Festival Theatre is laid on Wagner's fifty-ninth birthday, 22 May.

1874 On 28 April the Wagners move into the house 'Wahnfried' designed by Richard himself. The finishing of the score of *Götterdämmerung* on 21 November means the final completion of the *Ring*, which he had started on 4 October 1848.

1876 For a fee of 5,000 dollars Wagner composes a 'Festival March for the celebrations of the centenary of American independence'. On 13 August the first Bayreuth Festival opens with a performance of *Rheingold* produced by Wagner and conducted by Hans Richter. It is followed on 14 August by *Walküre* and by the first performances of *Siegfried* and *Götterdämmerung* on the 16 and 17 August respectively.

1877 Wagner gives eight concerts in the Albert Hall, London, and is received by Queen Victoria at Windsor Castle.

1882 Completion of the score of *Parsifal* on 13 January; it is performed for the first time on 26 July in the Bayreuth Festival Theatre and fifteen more performances follow by 29 August conducted by Hermann Levi. At the last performance Wagner, for the only time in the Festival Theatre, seizes the baton during the third act and conducts himself.

1883 Wagner dies of a coronary paralysis at the Palazzo Vendramin in Venice on 13 February. He is buried on 18 February at 'Wahnfried' in Bayreuth.

Frontispiece: Richard Wagner in 1865. From a photograph by F. Hanfstaengl, Munich.

6 FIRST PAGE of the original manuscript of *Mein Leben*, the autobiography which Wagner began dictating to Cosima von Bülow on 17 July 1865. The manuscript was corrected by Wagner in his own hand. It was not published till 1910.

8 THE INN '*Zum roth und weissen Löwen*', the house in Leipzig in which Wagner was born, *Auf dem Brühl* No. 3. It was pulled down in 1885. (Deutsche Fotothek, Dresden)

9 JOHANNA ROSINE WAGNER, *née* Paetz (1774—1848), Wagner's mother, who on the death of her first husband Friedrich Wagner married Ludwig Geyer. Oil painting by Ludwig Geyer. (Wagner-Gedenkstätte, Bayreuth)

10 LUDWIG GEYER (1778—1821) enjoyed a considerable reputation in Leipzig and Dresden both as an actor and as a portrait-painter. He married Rosine Wagner in 1814, so becoming Richard Wagner's stepfather. Self-portrait.

11 CHRISTIAN THEODOR WEINLIG (1780—1842), a cantor at St Thomas's Church, Leipzig, who instructed Wagner in harmony and composition.

FRONTISPIECE of Wagner's first published composition, a Piano Sonata of 1831, dedicated to Theodor Weinlig.

12 WILHELMINE SCHRÖDER-DEVRIENT (1804—60), Wagner's 'Muse'. In Dresden she was the first Adriano, the first Senta, and the first Venus. Lithograph by F. Hanfstaengl. (Hist. Bildarchiv Handke)

13 PLAYBILL of Raupach's play *König Enzio*, which in 1832 was given a number of performances at the Royal Court Theatre in Leipzig. Wagner wrote the incidental music for it at the age of nineteen.

15 ORCHESTRAL SKETCH for the opera *Das Liebesverbot*. Wagner wrote his own libretto, based on Shakespeare's *Measure for Measure*. The work was given for the first time at Magdeburg in 1836, Wagner himself conducting. It was not a success.

16 THE THEATRE AT LAUCHSTÄDT, originally instigated by Goethe, where Heinrich Bethmann's Magdeburg Company was playing. Bethmann appointed Wagner his musical director in 1834.

17 THE MAGDEBURG THEATRE, the scene of the *Liebesverbot* fiasco of 1836.

18 A PICTURE OF WAGNER discovered only a few years ago at Würzburg, where Wagner started his theatrical career in 1834. It is the earliest known portrait of the composer.

19 MINNA PLANER, who was the 'leading tragédienne' of the Magdeburg Company when Wagner first met her. They were married in 1836.

20 THE *Stadttheater* at Riga: playbill of a performance of *Maria Stuart*, with Mme Wagner as guest-artist.

21 THE *Rule, Britannia Overture* composed at Riga in 1837 and first performed there on 2 March 1838.

23 GIACOMO MEYERBEER, the 'musical Pope' of Vienna, surrounded by his works: a contemporary representation. (Nissen Collection)

Notes

24 WAGNER'S FIRST ABODE in Paris, the house in the Rue de la Tonnellerie in which Molière is wrongly said to have been born (now 31 rue du Pont-Neuf).

25 RICHARD AND MINNA'S HOTEL BILL, including a charge for the dog Robber.

26 AN ARRANGEMENT of a piece by Donizetti for the firm of Schlesinger by whom Wagner was employed.

27 A LETTER OF APOLOGY from Richard to Minna in the form of a poem, signed with a self-caricature done during the Paris days.

28 *Gazette Musicale: Pilgerfahrt zu Beethoven*, the story of a German musician, by Richard Wagner. It was this story that first made the musical world of Paris aware of Wagner.

29 WAGNER IN PARIS in 1842. Pencil drawing by Ernst Benedikt Kietz, Wagner's comrade during the years of privation.

30 THE ROYAL COURT THEATRE in Dresden at which *Rienzi*, the *Flying Dutchman* and *Tannhäuser* were performed for the first time. Woodcut (1843). (Hist. Bildarchiv Handke)

31 PLAYBILL of the first performance of *Rienzi* on 20 October 1842.

FRONTISPIECE of Wagner's occasional composition *At Weber's Grave*. It was at Wagner's instigation that Weber's body was brought from London to Dresden, where Weber had been Wagner's predecessor from 1817—25 in the post of Kapellmeister.

33 FARMSTEAD AT GRAUPA (Saxon Switzerland). It was here that the prose sketch of *Lohengrin* was completed in 1845. (Deutsche Fotothek, Dresden)

34 STAGE-SET for the first performance of the *Flying Dutchman*. Woodcut from the *Leipziger Illustrierte Zeitung* 1843, No. 15, which also published the music of the Sailors' Chorus.

THE *Flying Dutchman:* playbill of the first performance at Dresden on 2 January 1843.

35 JOSEPH TICHATSCHEK as Tannhäuser and Wilhelmine Schröder-Devrient as Venus: scene from the first performance at Dresden on 19 October 1845. Drawing by Th. Tischbein.

PLAYBILL of the first performance of *Tannhäuser*.

JOHANNA WAGNER, a niece of Richard's, sang the part of Elisabeth at the first performance.

36 THE INN AT TEPLITZ-SCHÖNAU, 'Zur Eiche', in which parts of *Tannhäuser* and practically all the sketches of the later works were evolved.

37 WAGNER'S ARRANGEMENT of Gluck. He also arranged Palestrina's *Stabat Mater* for a performance at Dresden.

38 MICHAEL ALEXANDER BAKUNIN (1814—76), one of the original founders of communism, was condemned to death for his rôle of ringleader in the Dresden May uprising but later extradited to Russia. He died in Bern in 1876. (Hist. Bildarchiv Handke)

39 THE WARRANT for Wagner's arrest, made out in Dresden on 16 May 1849. It applied not only to Saxony, but to all other German States.

41 FRANZ LISZT (1811—86) directed the Weimar Court Theatre for many years, and it was there that he conducted on 28 August 1850 the first performance of *Lohengrin*. Lithograph by C. Hoffmann.

42 RICHARD WAGNER in 1853. Lithograph by F. Hanfstaengl from a watercolour by Clementine Stockar-Escher. (Hist. Bildarchiv Handke)

43 TWO STAGE DESIGNS for *Lohengrin* by Wagner himself. They were intended for the first performance at Weimar, which Wagner was unable to attend owing to the warrant for his arrest.

44 SKETCH FOR THE DRAMA *Wieland the Smith*. The unfinished libretto contains a number of striking anticipations of the *Ring*.

45 THE FORMER *Aktientheater* in Zürich where in 1852 Wagner prepared and conducted a production of the *Flying Dutchman*. Lithograph.

46 OTTO WESENDONCK (1815—96), the silk-merchant who for many years was Wagner's friend and patron.

47 MATHILDE WESENDONCK (1828—1902), *née* Luckemeyer. Oil painting by C. Dörner.

48 MINNA WAGNER with her little dog Peps. Watercolour (1853) by Clementine Stockar-Escher.

49 THE WESENDONCKS' VILLA near Zürich where Wagner was often the centre of prominent gatherings.

THE *Album-Sonata* for Mathilde Wesendonck was the second work — the first being a *Polka* — that Wagner dedicated to his 'soul-mate'.

50 THE 'ASYL', a small cottage in the grounds of the Wesendoncks' villa, where Wagner sketched the first act of *Tristan* (October-December 1857).

51 IN THE WORKS of Arthur Schopenhauer (1788—1860) Wagner found a close correspondence to his own views of life.

53 FAIR COPY OF THE SCORE of *Tristan*. It is the chord in the second bar, a chord that defies strict harmonic analysis, that ushered in a whole new world of impressionism in music.

54 VENICE. It was in the Palazzo Giustiniani that on 18 March 1859 Wagner finished the second act of *Tristan*. Photograph from about 1860. (Hist. Bildarchiv Handke)

55 PRINCESS PAULINE METTERNICH, *née* Gräfin Sandór (1836—1921) wife of the Austrian Ambassador in Paris, Richard Metternich. She intervened with Napoleon to bring about the Paris performance of *Tannhäuser*. (Hist. Bildarchiv Handke)

56 TITLE PAGE OF '*Zukunftsmusik*' (the music of the future), an open letter from Wagner to a French friend of his, Fr. Villot, being a 'Preface to a prose translation of his opera libretti'.

57 'WAGNER punctures the ear-drums of his audience'. A caricature by Gill in *Eclipse,* 18 April 1869.

58 *Tannhäuser* poster in Paris. The first performance of the Paris version in the Grand Opera House on 13 March 1861 ended in an unprecedented uproar.

59 ALBERT NIEMANN (1831—1917) as Tannhäuser in the Paris production. Later Wagner engaged him for Bayreuth, where he sang the part of Siegmund in 1876.

60 WAGNER'S OWN ALTERATIONS to the Prize-Song in the libretto of *Die Meistersinger*. He found the original version too jejune.

61 MATHILDE MAIER (1834—1910), daughter of a Wiesbaden lawyer, was one of Wagner's most loyal friends and remained his confidante right up to the 'Wahnfried' days.

62 FRIEDERIKE MEYER, sister of the Luise Dustmann who was ear-marked for the part of Isolde in Vienna. Friederike left Frankfurt to join Wagner in Vienna, where she enjoyed his favour for a while.

63 SKETCH FOR THE APARTMENT at Penzing, a suburb of Vienna. The fittings cost a fortune, and in March 1864 Wagner was forced to give the slip to his creditors. In May of the same year he was summoned to the Court of King Ludwig II of Bavaria, who generously enabled him to pay off his most pressing debts.

64 *Huldigungsmarsch* (Homage March) for King Ludwig II, performed for the first time on 5 October 1864 in the courtyard of the Munich Residenz. Autograph.

65 KING LUDWIG II OF BAVARIA (1845—86), who was bound to Wagner by close ties of friendship and adulation and shortly after ascending the throne summoned him to Munich. (Süddeutscher Verlag, Bildarchiv)

66 WAGNER at the age of fifty-two. After a photograph by F. Hanfstaengl, Munich.

67 MODEL of a proposed Festival Theatre at Munich by Gottfried Semper. It was on Wagner's suggestion that the Dresden architect was summoned to Munich by Ludwig. The project eventually came to nothing.

68 PROSE SKETCH for *Parsifal* (Parzifal) written in August 1865 for Ludwig II; and a sketch from a drama about Buddha entitled *Die Sieger*.

69 WAGNER'S RESIDENCE in Munich at Briennerstrasse 21, not far from the Residenz. The house was destroyed during World War II.

70 AFTER THE REHEARSAL of *Tristan* in 1865: Wagner escorts Cosima through the streets of Munich while Hans von Bülow follows with the music. Drawing by M. Schultze. (Adi Gerhauser, Munich)

71 HANS VON BÜLOW (1830—94), an ardent admirer of Wagner and first husband of Cosima Liszt. He conducted the first performances of *Tristan* and *Die Meistersinger* at Munich.

72 LUDWIG AND MALWINA SCHNORR VON CAROLSFELD: scene from the first performance of *Tristan* on 10 June 1865.

73 BIRGIT NILSSON and Wolfgang Windgassen in a performance of *Tristan* at Bayreuth in 1957 produced by Wolfgang Wagner.

74 KING LUDWIG'S LETTER ordering Wagner not to leave Munich, written on 11 March 1865. In December of the same year, however, the King, yielding to pressure from his Parliament, was forced to instruct Wagner to depart.

75 A PORTRAIT OF WAGNER by Franz Lenbach, one of his many portraits of Richard and Cosima.

76 THE HOUSE AT TRIEBSCHEN where Wagner lived from 15 April 1866 till 22 April 1872. (Franz Schneider, Lucerne)

77 FRANZ LISZT (1811—86) with his daughter Cosima von Bülow (1837—1930). Her mother was Countess Marie d'Agoult.

78 WAGNER IN OLD GERMAN COSTUME with his daughter Eva, born in 1867. It was only at home that Wagner wore this costume: he designed the cap himself from pictures by Rembrandt.

79 AFTER THE FIRST PERFORMANCE of *Die Meistersinger* at Munich: Wagner expressing his gratitude to the audience from the royal box. Tinted pen and ink drawing by Joseph Resch.

80 AUTOGRAPH OF A PLAY called *Luthers Hochzeit* that Wagner was planning in the summer of 1868.

81 RICHARD AND COSIMA IN 1874.

The announcement of Wagner's wedding: he married Cosima five years after Minna's death, on 25 August 1870 in the Protestant Church at Lucerne.

82 FRIEDRICH NIETZSCHE (1844–1900) was first introduced to Wagner in 1868 at the Leipzig home of the latter's brother-in-law, Heinrich Brockhaus.

83 HANS RICHTER (1843–1916), Wagner's invaluable assistant, especially with the *Ring*. In 1876 he conducted the first performance of the *Ring* in Bayreuth.

THE LETTER from Rubinstein: 'I am a Jew'. Joseph Rubinstein — no relation to the pianist Anton — was the 'family' pianist at 'Wahnfried'. After Wagner's death he committed suicide.

85 STAGE-SET for the first performance of *Rheingold* at Munich on 22 September 1869. Wagner ostentatiously stayed away from this disastrous performance commanded by Ludwig II.

86 THE MARGRAVES' OPERA HOUSE at Bayreuth, built in 1747, and fitted out by Giuseppe and Carlo Bibiena, was the largest German theatre of its day.

87 THE DEEDS OF CONVEYANCE from the Municipality of Bayreuth, by which Wagner was presented free of charge with a site for a Festival Theatre. The purchase price, 14,000 gulden, was found by the Municipality 'in view of the importance of the project'.

88 PROGRAMME of the ceremonial laying of the foundation-stone at Bayreuth, the climax of which was a performance of Beethoven's Ninth Symphony, with Wagner conducting, in the Margraves' Opera House on 22 May 1872, for the especial benefit of the Festival's patrons.

89 THE FESTIVAL THEATRE, Bayreuth, in 1876, when the *Ring* was first performed. The actual building was supervised by Otto Brückwald, but the design was Wagner's own, based on experiences in his Kapellmeister days at Riga.

THE FESTIVAL THEATRE in construction on 2 August 1873.

90 LUDWIG II'S DECLARATION of patronage. It was a credit of 100,000 taler from the King that enabled the Festival Theatre to be completed.

A VIEW OF THE ORCHESTRA PIT during a rehearsal of *Parsifal* in 1882, showing Wagner's own placing of the various instruments. From a cubby-hole behind the conductor, Hermann Levi, Wagner issues instructions.

91 INTERIOR OF THE 'Wagner-theatre' during a performance of *Rheingold*. Sketch by L. Bechstein.

92 THE 'MACHINERY' FOR *Rheingold:* the Rhine Maidens are strapped into baskets mounted on a movable structure invisible to the audience, to whom the figures seem to be floating and swimming.

93 MINNA LAMMERT, Lilli and Marie Lehmann, the Rhine Maidens at the 1876 Bayreuth Festival.

94 FRANZ BETZ AS WOTAN and Joseph Nierung as Hunding in *Walküre* at the 1876 Bayreuth Festival. (Original photographs)

95 EIGHTY YEARS LATER: Hans Hotter as Wotan in Wieland Wagner's production.

96 GEORG UNGER as Siegfried, an original photograph of the 1876 production of *Götterdämmerung*.

BERND ALDENHOFF as the young Siegfried in Wieland Wagner's production at Bayreuth in 1951.

Notes 97 THE RIDE OF THE VALKYRIES at Bayreuth in 1876, on a structure drawn across a background from left to right. (Wagner-Gedenkstätte, Bayreuth)

98 BRÜNNHILDE'S AWAKENING: a contemporary reproduction from the 1876 Bayreuth production.

99 BRÜNNHILDE'S AWAKENING in Wieland Wagner's 1957 production.

100 COSIMA WAGNER at the age of twenty-eight. (A contemporary photograph)

101 RICHARD WAGNER, after an oil painting by Hubert von Herkomer, 1877.

102, 103 'Wahnfried', Bayreuth. Part of the 'Halle' with the bust of Siegfried Wagner; a corner of the 'Saal' with Wagner's desk and Lenbach's portrait of Schopenhauer; and Cosima's 'lilac salon' with Lenbach's portraits of Wagner and Liszt. The house was designed by Wagner himself and financed by King Ludwig. The Wagners moved in on 28 April 1874. The garden façade was demolished by shellfire during World War II, and the famous music-room was completely wrecked.

104, 105 A RECEPTION AT 'Wahnfried': in front, left, Siegfried with Cosima Wagner, Amalie Materna and Richard Wagner: behind, Franz von Lenbach, Emil Scaria, Fr. Fischer, Fritz Brand and Hermann Levi. At the piano, Franz Liszt, with Hans Richter, Franz Betz and Albert Niemann. In front, right, Gräfin Schleinitz, Gräfin Usedom and Paul von Joukowsky. After an oil painting by Papperitz.

106 A FAMILY PORTRAIT: Cosima, Richard and Siegfried Wagner.

107 AT THE ANGERMANN INN, which Wagner frequently patronised for a 'sundowner'. On Wagner's right, the singer Albert Niemann: on his left Dr Eugen Gura. (Hist. Bildarchiv Handke)

108 'APOTHEOSIS': Caricature from the Vienna publication *Bombe*, 2 September 1876

THE MASTER'S OWN WORDS to Amalie Materna: 'Stiflingly hot today! What about a sponge down, Madame?' Caricature in *Junger Kikeriki*, Vienna 1882

108, 109 CARICATURE in *Figaro*, Vienna, 1870: Richard Wagner; 'Thankyou, Mr Night Watchman, for lighting me on my way into the future'. Night Watchman Dingelstedt (Director of the Vienna Opera); 'Mind you don't come a cropper!'

WAGNER and the head of the publishing house of Schott. Pencil caricature.

109 WAGNER as a composer: caricature in the *Illustrated Sporting and Dramatic News*, London, 9 June 1877

CARICATURE in *Kikeriki*, Vienna 1876: 'Wagner gets all the unwanted drums in the Austrian Ministry of War.'

110 BISMARCK'S reply to the poem Wagner sent him, '*To the German army at the gates of Paris*'.

111 THE *Romeo and Juliet* theme which Wagner planned in honour of those who died in the Franco-Prussian war of 1870–71.

112 WAGNER was a great lover of animals, and wrote a passionate tract against vivisection and all other forms of cruelty to animals. A petition bearing his signature among others was, on Virchow's instructions, not debated in the *Reichstag*.

113 WAGNER, the musician of the future. Caricature in *La sifflet*, 27 August 1876

114 JUDITH GAUTIER (1850–1917), daughter of the French writer Théophile Gautier, was herself a writer and later described her relationship with Wagner.

115 THE *Parsifal* theme which Wagner wrote down specially for Judith Gautier.

THE PRODUCTION OF *Parsifal:* from left to right, Paul von Joukowsky (décor), Hermann Levi (conductor) and Karl Brandt (stage-manager).

116 THE FINAL PAGE OF THE SCORE OF *Parsifal*, with the dedication to Cosima of 25 December 1881. The eleven immediately preceding pages were not completed till 1882. Wagner had devised a method whereby the incomplete pages could be filled in later.

117 PARSIFAL (Hermann Winkelmann) and the Flower Maidens at the 1882 Bayreuth production.

THÉRÈSE MALTEN as Kundry (1882): a scene from the second act.

118 THE GRAAL TEMPLE that Paul von Joukowsky designed for the 1882 performances was still being used at Bayreuth in the 1930's.

119 THE GRAAL TEMPLE for the new production of *Parsifal* at the 1951 Bayreuth Festival, designed by Wieland Wagner.

120 THE *Adagio* theme of a projected symphony (?) dated 2 March 1882.

121 AUGUSTE RENOIR painted this portrait of Wagner in 1884 from a sketch made two years earlier at Palermo.

122 WAGNER'S LAST ABODE, the Palazzo Vendramin in Venice. Today the Palazzo houses an Italian Radio station.

123 IN FRONT OF THE Palazzo Vendramin: Cosima and Richard, now almost seventy.

124 THIS PENCIL SKETCH was made by Paul von Joukowsky in Cosima's diary while Wagner was reading aloud Fouqué's *Undine* on the evening before his death.

THE LAST LINES of the article on 'The female element in human nature'; at the final words '*Liebe-Tragik*' the pencil slipped from his grasp.

125 THE SOFA on which Wagner died. The rest of the furniture in the Palazzo Vendramin apartment was burned at Cosima's wish. (Wagner-Gedenkstätte, Bayreuth)

126 THE ARRIVAL OF THE CORTÈGE in Munich. Woodcut after a drawing by L. Bechstein. (Archiv Winkler, Brunswick)

THE PROGRAMME of the funeral at Bayreuth on 18 February 1883.

127 THE FUNERAL PROCESSION passing through the streets of Bayreuth. Contemporary woodcut. (Archiv Winkler, Brunswick)

128 WAGNER'S DEATH-MASK, made by the Italian sculptor Augusto Benvenuti. (W. v Poswik, Landshut)

In all cases where the source is not quoted, the pictures are from the 'Wahnfried' archives at Bayreuth.

Bibliography

ERNEST NEWMAN. *The Life of Richard Wagner* (4 vols). 1933–47.

WAGNER, RICHARD. *My Life* (2 vols). 1911 (translation of his autobiography *Mein Leben*).

WAGNER, RICHARD. *Letters of Richard Wagner.* Selected and edited by Wilhelm Altmann; translated by M. M. Bozman (2 vols). 1927.

This version of Wagner's life is based primarily on Curt von Westenhagen's book on Wagner published by Atlantis-Verlag, as well as on Wagner's own writings and autobiography. Among other works consulted were *Richard Wagner: Briefe 1835–1865* (the Burrell Collection), S. Fischer Verlag, 1953; Zdenko von Kraft's *Richard Wagner*, Andermann-Verlag; Joachim von Kürenberg's *Karneval der Einsamen*, Robert Mölch-Verlag, Hamburg, 1947; and Sophie Rützow's *Richard Wagner in Bayreuth*, Verlag Ulrich & Co., Nürnberg.

Extensive use has been made of Wagner's correspondence, primarily with the King of Bavaria (G. Braun, Karlsruhe, 1937), but also with Minna Wagner, Otto and Mathilde Wesendonck, Mathilde Maier, Hans von Bülow, Franz Liszt, Judith Gautier, Eliza Wille, Julie Ritter, etc.

Much essential information has been taken from the Bayreuth Festival programmes published annually since 1951.

The biographical details, such as dates of journeys and performances, are based on the chronological table published by the Bayreuth Festival authorities and compiled with extraordinary accuracy by Otto Strobel, who corrects a number of mistakes by earlier Wagner biographers. Both the author and the publishers are deeply indebted to Frau Winifred Wagner for her kindness in making available a number of hitherto virtually unknown documents as well as for permission to publish copies of the pictures.

INDEX OF NAMES

Numbers in italics refer to the illustrations